SAMPLE
SOCIAL
SPEECHES

'A vessel is known by the sound, whether it is cracked or not, so men are proved by their speeches whether they be wise or foolish.'

Demosthenes.

SAMPLE SOCIAL SPEECHES

WIT
STORIES, JOKES
ANECDOTES, EPIGRAMS

by

GORDON WILLIAMS

PAPERFRONTS
ELLIOT RIGHT WAY BOOKS
KINGSWOOD, SURREY, U.K.

Elliot Right Way Books MCMLXVI
Completely revised and largely re-written
edition, re-set, © Elliot Right Way Books MCMLXXXIII
Reprinted MCMLXXXVI

Printed and bound in Great Britain by
Hartnolls Ltd., Bodmin, Cornwall

Dedicated to
David Lloyd Hughes, who likens a
speech to a bicycle wheel – the longer
the spoke the bigger the tyre!

Contents

Foreword

It is hoped that this book will help you not only to prepare pleasant, amusing speeches, but, also, to quell some of the terror which everyone experiences when he is first asked to speak in public.

While the book is primarily intended for the busy person, who has neither the time nor the inclination to make a deep, intensive study of the art of public speaking, it contains much that even the most practised of public speakers will find useful.

Part 1 shows one how to prepare and deliver a speech with the least possible trouble and effort. It does so in simple language, is unpretentious, and certainly does not blind one with science!

Parts 2 and 3 contain samples of speeches which cover practically every social occasion upon which you might be asked to stand up and say a few words. In the main, these speeches are amusing, and, when properly delivered, raise laughter. And laughter, in its proper place, is a joy and encouragement to every speaker.

You can use these speeches as they are, or, maybe, you will decide to select parts from two or more of them, and with these, form a new speech, which you might consider more individualistic to your occasion.

Part 4 contains anecdotes, aphorisms and stories which you can use to refurbish one of the sample speeches which appear earlier, or, you may decide, with their aid, to prepare an entirely new speech which will have the merit of being your own work, and, consequently, will be much more personal.

A number of the speeches which appear in Part 3 were delivered as after-dinner speeches when I was the principal speaker. Others were formal replies to specific toasts, such as 'Our Guests,' on the occasion of some dinner held by an organisation. The remainder have been specially written for this book.

In every instance, the gist of what one says in a social speech is the same: Thank you for asking me; Your organisation is admirable; You are doing excellent work; Please continue with it; I wish you the very best of good luck.

Indeed, these sentiments are the bare bones of ninety per cent of all the after-dinner speeches which are made. But delivered in that form they occupy about one minute from start to finish, and provide little pleasure for the audience, who will make sure that the poor unfortunate who offers them, just like that, will never be invited again.

These days, audiences expect a speaker to be on his feet for about ten minutes, and during this period it is his job to hold the attention and interest of his listeners. To do this, what we have called the bare bones of a speech have to be unified.

They have to be put together so that they have form – a beginning, a middle and an end. Then the 'form' must be made to live with stories, anecdotes and aphorisms.

When a speaker has done his work well he will sit down with the sweet sound of applause ringing in his ears, and far from saying to himself, 'Never Again!' he will be looking forward to his listeners saying, 'Please come again.'

PART I

Constructing A
Social Speech

Every social or other speech requires three separate parts: a beginning, a middle and an end. In other words introduction, development and conclusion.

The beginning should capture the attention of the audience and introduce the subject. The middle is its development or exposition. Here the audience is told what you want it to know and how it is affected. You may lecture, preach or explain. But speak brightly no matter what the occasion. The end is not just finishing, nor a trailing off – rather a well-considered rounding off which leaves the audience feeling satisfied with a speech to be remembered.

On social occasions we don't normally lecture, preach or explain. Sometimes we congratulate, but usually we welcome guests or say thank you for your hospitality.

It would be easy if we could congratulate, welcome or thank people adding a word on the future. But tradition demands that we devote long moments to saying these things. This is where the agony may come in perhaps especially for the audience!

Let us study the matter.

The Beginning

Aim to hook your audience. This is easy when you begin your career because being an unknown and inexperienced speaker your audience will be agog with interest. This fortunately lasts until it becomes known that you are competent. After that you will have to work on your audience like a professional entertainer.

The novice or unknown speaker is safe in starting speeches with thanks to the organization for their invitation and hospitality.

When you are known you will have to employ the professional's devices for capturing your audience. Four of these are now described.

1. Ask A Question

Start by asking your audience a question, which must, of course, be relevant to your subject or to them. You could begin a speech at a social club thus: 'Can any of you tell me what happiness is?' Then pause a moment, to let your question sink in and to allow your audience to collect their thoughts. Next you could continue: 'Of course many of you can tell me what happiness is. The happy look on your faces assures me of this. Finding words to express happiness is something one might find a little difficult though. I read recently that happiness is being satisfied with what you have got as well as with what you haven't got. A friend of mine put it this way: 'Happiness is a wayside station between those two great termini, Too Little and Too Much.'

'This club of yours seems to me to have a great deal to do with keeping open that wayside station . . .' and so on.

A variation of this beginning is to get your audience to ask questions of themselves. For instance: 'This audience has got something one does not always come across at gatherings such as this. Standing here I can both feel and see it. Feel it because every public speaker forms a bond with the audience he is addressing. See it because it is written on your faces . . . ! What is this I feel and see? It is your happiness . . .' and so on.

2. Start With a Quotation

Imagine you are addressing a tennis club. Start by saying:

'Birds of a feather flock together.' Before you are half-way through your audience will be quoting with you willy-nilly. You will have caught their attention. Their thoughts are now focused on you and what you have to say. Pause a moment or two after your quotation and then go on to make it an integral part of your speech. For instance: 'Birds of a feather flock together. When I was at school I frequently heard this proverb quoted. But never in a complimentary sense. Always it was after two or more of us had been misbehaving. By now I have had experience enough of life to realize that my mentors did not know everything and that this proverb can be used to describe all kinds of organizations.

'What are we here tonight but birds of a feather? The "feather" common to us all being a devotion to tennis. In the fourteenth century it was known as the Game of Kings. Charles V of France actually forbade his subjects to play it . . .' and so forth.

3. Say Something Which Is A Complete Denial of The Views You Are Known to Hold

The audience gets such a surprise at hearing you uttering such a heresy that it is shocked into listening. For example, supposing you are addressing a golf club, start: 'Golf is a good walk spoilt . . .!' Pause a moment to let what you have said sink in, then add: 'So said that great American author Mark Twain . . .' Now carry on with the body of your speech.

4. Tell a Relevant Story

This should not be a funny story because the art of getting a laugh out of an audience within a moment of starting a speech is most difficult. Even professional comedians find it hard to get their first laugh. It has something to do with an audience needing time to warm up.

Suppose you are addressing a motoring organization;

'Recently a remarkable bus driver retired. In all the years he had been employed by the bus company he had never been involved in an accident. His colleagues agreed to give him a farewell party and the bus company decided that their manager should present him with a specially struck gold medal and a mantelpiece clock.

'On the night of the party the manager referred in glowing terms to the driver's record and presented him with his awards.

'Presently the driver had to reply. He did so in words something like these: "I'm no great shakes at making speeches but I suppose you all want to know how I managed all these years without an accident. Well, it's like this. There's only one way to do it. Drive like everyone else on the road was plumb crazy!'

'Undoubtedly that is splendid advice. If everyone followed it then the roads would be much safer places. I hope everyone in this organization takes it to heart ...!' and so forth.

Aesop's fables provide a source for anecdotes of this kind. Assume you are addressing a club function.

'One of Aesop's fables tells the story of a big dog and a donkey which set off on a long journey.

'The donkey had a heavy load of bread on his back and stopped after a while to eat grass from the hedgerow.

'"I'm hungry too," complained the dog. "Please give me a piece of bread."

'"I'm sorry," replied the donkey coldly. "I can't spare any of it. If you want to eat you must do like me – find something by the wayside."

'And so the poor dog had to do without any food.

'They walked on until presently they espied a wolf in the distance. At once the donkey began to tremble. "You're not going to run away are you, Dog?" he whined. "You'll stay and help me won't you?"

'"I'm sorry," said the dog, "but those who eat alone will have to fight alone. Good-bye." And he left the greedy donkey to fend for himself.

'Well, you in this club are not like that donkey. You have long ago discovered that the secret of friendship, companionship and co-operation is to be friendly, companionable and co-operative. It is because you realize this that you are members of this club.' ... and so on.

The Middle

If we were concerned with a speech other than a social speech this would be the longest section. I would show how to expound your theme and put across your message. This would be where you lectured, preached or explained.

You would be told to find suitable sub-headings. You would be shown how to deal with these one by one, and how to illustrate each in turn by quotations, personal experiences, anecdotes or stories all helping to fix points in the minds of your listeners.

You would be told to demonstrate, as you dealt with them, how each of your sub-headings affected your audience.

We are, however, concerned with social speeches and all you usually do in these is congratulate, welcome or thank.

Do so as interestingly as possible, using anecdotes and amusing stories to enliven what you say.

Appropriate new stories are invaluable. Therefore when you happen to come across one record it. You never know when it will illuminate one of your speeches. Because it lessens the difficulty in indexing, I record mine in a loose-leaf memo book, adding pages to each section as required.

Some page-a-day calendars contain a thought for each day. Try to acquire one and add the aphorisms and stories that appeal to you to your collection.

No story or joke is appropriate to every occasion. Care and ingenuity are often needed in thinking up ways of introducing them so that they don't sound out of place but form an integral part of your speech.

In this the middle part of your speech, include words of praise for the organization you are attending. Praise is a kind of spiritual vitamin, a precious plus in life. Lord Chesterfield said: 'I never knew any man deserve praise, who did not desire it.'

It is permissible in a social speech to include details of how the organization started and its principles. But get your facts right first. Make one mistake and you'll find every member of your audience was listening!

The End

The end is an integral part of your speech. It completes it. Don't end with a jerk. If this were other than a social speech you would summarize, tie up any loose ends, and try to get some action following what you had said. With a social speech, however, you merely repeat your thanks, wish the organization and its members good luck and perhaps with a great brotherhood remind the brethren of the principles which bind them together.

I always find it effective to finish off with a story.

The specimen speeches in Part 3, suitably adapted, will cover any social occasion. If the organization is one about which you know little have a talk with its secretary or another knowledgeable member. They will supply you with all the information you need, so that on the day you will sound erudite. Members take it as a compliment if you show you have some knowledge of their affairs. And in a social speech one of your hopes is that you please your listeners and obtain their applause.

Delivering Your Speech

Before my first public speech a friend advised me: Stand up so that your audience can see you, speak up so that your audience can hear you then sit down so that your audience can enjoy themselves. I stood up. Immediately, my heart pounded, my legs went rubbery and a mist came before my eyes. I began: 'Mr Chairman, ladies and gentlemen,' and was at once breathless. I felt suffocated and in misery I floundered on, missing much of what I intended saying, until at last it was over. I sat down exhausted, enjoying the fact that I had finished far more than my audience, which to my surprise, cheered; but the cheers seemed far off!

Never again, I vowed, but the gods willed otherwise. I was soon undergoing the same torture with the prospect of more doses to come.

What follows is the result of my researches into ways of improving the position. Today, far from being terror-stricken when I make a speech, I enjoy the experience.

The secret is to PREPARE. Every good public speaker prepares. Those spontaneous speeches you admire have usually taken hours or days of preparation. The late Sir Winston Churchill, one of the greatest public speakers of all time, whose speeches galvanized Britain in the hour of need, prepared assiduously. The novice must do his homework if he wishes to succeed.

With a little adaptation to the specimen speeches given later almost every occasion can be covered. This is true even when making further speeches to the same audience on similar occasions.

To benefit from this book you should select your speech

then make your adaptations to improve it. Next, take it into an unoccupied room.

Stand in the room, feet twelve to fourteen inches apart, and balance your weight equally on them. This is the stance you should try to adopt when speaking. Hold your speech in front of you and read it aloud. The sound of your voice, this first time, may disconcert and embarrass you. Worse you may find my style and sentences difficult. If so, do a rewrite using your own phraseology. This will help because now there is something of yourself in it. Indeed it is always wiser to alter my samples to your own words for in that way you are identified with them.

Try to keep your sentences short. Before an audience you may find at first you become breathless. Short sentences are then easier and your audience will find them simpler to follow.

Make your speech a second time in the empty room. It should be easier.

If you are satisfied with the result, read it again, giving your voice the same volume as you would when you are to deliver it.

Speak slowly. This is important. New speakers rush too quickly. They tend to gabble and the effect is consequently lost. Go carefully, pausing for breath as required.

I do not recommend you at this stage to test on a tape-recorder. The majority of them do not faithfully reproduce your voice. Many of them give the impression that you speak slower than you do, so that afterwards you try to increase your speed. As a novice speaker, hurried speaking is something to guard against, not cultivate.

If you must hear your voice cup your hands round your ears and speak aloud. That is pretty much what your voice sounds like.

After several practice runs set about familiarizing yourself with your speech.

Some learn their speeches by heart and recite them on the night; others find this too much trouble and prefer to deliver either from the manuscript or from notes of its salient points. I take my manuscript with me, arguing that if national figures do this why shouldn't I.

I double-space my manuscript and am generous with paragraphing. When you come to read my specimen speeches you may think I have used too many paragraphs. But these are speeches, not mere pieces of writing. They have been set down so that on the night my eye can alight with ease on any line which evades my memory.

I go further. I underline paragraphs which gave me trouble in rehearsal, so that if they are elusive, on the night, my eye finds them and I am able to refresh my memory without searching for the place.

I find it useful to run over my speech in my mind before dropping off to sleep for a few nights before the date. This helps it to sink into the subconscious. In the morning I again run over it mentally. It is surprising the effect this has – learning becomes easy.

If you cannot do this with the whole speech do please try it with your stories. A well-told story will often turn a mediocre speech into a moderate success; your audience almost forgetting the black spots.

Between your first reading of your speech and its delivery on the night you should read it aloud alone, several times. If you can persuade anyone to listen to it that helps. Rehearse the speech properly before them; in the way you intend delivering it – standing up and employing whatever gestures or voice modulation you intend to use on the occasion.

With experience you will discover you can create effects with your voice by regulating the speed at which you speak and varying the tone.

Such techniques are practised by actors. Although I feel an after-dinner speaker is rather a cross between a lecturer and a music-hall comedian, it is beyond our scope to discuss this in detail. To learn more, listen to speakers on television and you will discover how professionals get their effects.

On the night look your smartest, and don't wear a row of

pens in your breast pocket, or anything which might distract attention from what you are saying.

When called upon to speak, stand up and push back your chair so that it doesn't press against you or interfere with the ease of your stance.

Place your feet twelve to fourteen inches apart for good balance as you did when you were rehearsing. Hold your speech in front of you, your thumbs in the margins. Take a deep breath, smile at your audience and start: 'Mr Chairman, ladies and gentlemen. ...'

As you progress work your thumbs down the page to indicate the place.

Consult your manuscript as often as you please, but do look round your audience, and try to project your voice so that it can be heard at the end of the room.

If the faces frighten you, imagine they each owe you £50, or silently, to yourself, call them fools – anything that gives you a feeling of superiority.

Should you get applause or laughter, pause till it is over. After a funny story, allow a moment for the normal reaction and pray to the Good Lord that it will come.

Try to avoid using your notes when telling a story. If you can't, consult your notes up to your punch line, but do ensure that you deliver that, looking at your audience.

Don't be tempted to wander from your manuscript. If you do, you will probably go astray and make a mess of trying to recover.

If you leave a bit of your speech out, don't worry; your audience may never notice.

Try to maintain the volume of your voice throughout so that your audience can hear every word. Try near the end to finish with something of a flourish. Then sit down at once.

I stare at the table for a moment after I have finished speaking. If there is a drink I help myself to a much-needed draught before once again looking at the people.

Try your speech out on a tape-recorder when you get home – if you want to. You will have time to get over its effects before you are called upon again!

If you are nervous before starting, remember so is every good speaker and actor. It is not until they are under way and lost in what they have to say that they forget themselves and their audience.

The Speeches

'My sermon on the meaning of manna in the wilderness can be adapted to almost any occasion, joyful, or, as in the present case, distressing. I have preached it at harvest celebrations, christenings, confirmations, on days of humiliation and festal days. The last time I delivered it was at the cathedral, as a charity sermon on behalf of the Society for the Prevention of Discontent among the Upper Orders. The Bishop, who was present, was much struck by some of the analogies I drew.'

So spoke Canon Chasuble in Oscar Wilde's *The Importance Of Being Ernest*.

The speeches which follow contain many epigrams, stories and anecdotes. These like a cat can have many lives and can like Canon Chasuble's sermon on the meaning of manna in the wilderness be adapted almost to any occasion.

As a number of epigrams, stories and anecdotes are contained in the specimen speeches, may I explain how I use the collection which follows?

Firstly, I gather all the information I can relative to the occasion upon which I am to speak, and write it down. This I call my preliminary information. Next I consult the indexes of this book and find if there is anything in them relevant to my preliminary information. If so I abstract it and add it to the information.

I then mull over all this, using my imagination. Eventually, I abstract from it what I think will convey what I have to say in an interesting and amusing fashion. From this I write my speech.

PART II

I
Speeches For The Best Man

If it were not for weddings many people would never be asked to make a speech.

In the next few chapters are speeches for the best man, the bride's father and the bridegroom. Frequently, a friend of the bride's family speaks instead of its head – and so there are some speeches for him, as well as for the bridegroom's father who occasionally speaks.

They contain epigrams and stories. By transferring these from one speech to another the average person should have ample material for all the weddings at which he may have to speak. Additional stories will be found at the end of the book.

Best Man's Speech No. 1.

I wonder if anybody at this wedding knows why I am called the Best Man? Surely the best man here today is the Bridegroom. It is his day, not mine. I am here to look after him until he departs on his honeymoon. And after that I have the delightful duty of looking after the bridesmaids.

Things were not always so. Generations ago, the best man had to marry the bride if the groom failed to attend the wedding. In those days his title was, in my opinion, more appropriate, he was then called the second-best man.

I have not discovered why this custom fell into disuse. Maybe too many bachelors refused to become second-best men. Or perhaps brides-to-be found those who risked it were almost always unsuitable, and caused a scene.

I suppose though, that the first of these reasons is the true one, for isn't a bachelor a man who tries to avoid the issue?

But I am not a confirmed bachelor. I don't think that the only marriage which can be justified is the one which produced me. I approve of this one today and wish Jack and Jill every good luck.

I approve of their marriage for another reason too. Haven't they made me their best man? And haven't I, in consequence, the pleasure of looking after these charming bridesmaids?

Our bride looks beautiful, and Jack already looks the dutiful husband. The two will always remember this day, and, from time to time, will think about all of us who are here, making it the wonder that it is.

We wish you, Jack and Jill, the best in health, wealth and happiness – and when you come to consider your next big investment together, may we hopefully point out that there's nothing like putting your money in – livestock!

Ladies and gentlemen, I ask you to rise and drink, with me, the toast of the Bride and Groom.

Best Man's Speech No. 2

I am enjoying this wedding. Everything has gone as smooth as clockwork. The wicked fairies have kept away. Instead it has been fairy-godmothers and magic all the way.

And amidst such beauty! Everyone is either in their Sunday best or a very special wedding outfit – enchanting, radiant! Say what you will, but fine feathers do make fine birds, don't they?

The bride and bridesmaids are the prettiest of pictures.

Indeed, many have been taken of them, and, like you, I have made sure of getting copies. It is the loveliest of days.

Everyone is happy. Even those of us who have speeches to make.

The bridegroom looks super too, doesn't he? Until I handed him the ring in Church he was my responsibility you know. Now Jill has him, and I have prettier charges than him – our bridesmaids. Admire them – there is no extra charge.

Beautiful, aren't they? They are my responsibility and I am their chief escort. Best man's perks you know! I am delighted with them ... Purring like a pussy-cat.

We are enjoying ourselves so much – they and I – that we beg you Jack and Jill, to invite us to all your other weddings. We've decided that you must have two at least, perhaps three. You both seem strong and fit enough for the course. I am not advocating bigamy but am referring to anniversaries – silver, ruby and golden weddings, of course. At those we hope that little strangers will have multiplied into second and third generations; more if Jack and Jill get on with it and don't waste time.

And if you're ever in need of baby-sitters, try us – your bridesmaids and best man, we're hopeful and willing.

And now it is my most pleasant duty to reply to the toast to the bridesmaids, charmingly proposed by Jack and so enthusiastically received by you. Our bridesmaids have greatly enjoyed being here and meeting all of you. They are grateful to each and all of you for making them so welcome and the day itself a perfect day.

Thank you all very much.

Best Man's Speech No. 3

When Jack asked me to be his best man and I said Yes, I didn't know that the best man had to make a speech. Well I'm a bachelor and have kept away from weddings. Nobody told me about the speech-making until last week. It was too late then for me to do anything about it.

A week before the invitations went out, I might have managed to persuade Jack to get Jill to elope. That way no one would have to undergo the tortures of making or listening to speeches.

But then we wouldn't be having this do either. Moreover Jack and Jill wouldn't be getting wedding presents. Gifts by which to remember their friends and this wonderful day would not be on.

Can't win, can we?

I think Jack is in all fairness bound to say that, unaccustomed as I am to these things, I've coped with all my best man's duties pretty well. Well, nothing has actually gone wrong, that is, yet, anyway, and I'm keeping my fingers crossed, not only me but Jack too.

So maybe you'll let me off this speechifying hook lightly and not expect too many words from me.

You nice people don't really want to hear me at all, I'm sure. It's this bogey called convention that's the trouble. This doing things proper!

We all came to witness the joining together of Jack and Jill, the making of two into one, and touchingly beautiful it was. We also all came to wish this worthy union everything that is fine, good, desirable and happy.

And no one wishes this more fervently than the bridesmaids and myself. Jack said some very nice things about them as he asked you to drink to their health and happiness, and it is now my pleasant duty on their behalf to reply to him.

The bridesmaids are very glad to be here today. They much appreciate the kind things you have said about their work and their looks. They say that it is good to know that they have given everybody pleasure besides giving satisfactory service to dear Jill who they think makes a stunning bride.

Their wish and mine is that the bride and groom may have a long and happy life, and, too, that all of you here today

may long be spared to remember them and this happy day.
Thank you one and all.

*For someone who is nervous and wants to get his speech
finished as soon as he may decently do so, this can be
effective.*

Best Man's Speech No. 4

Making speeches, as most of you nice people here know, is
not my favourite rôle. On the contrary the very thought of
making one terrifies me – gives me nerves, stomach troubles
and upsets me all over. Whenever people try to inflict such a
rôle upon me I reply at once with a point blank, No! Too
often I even forget to say thank you for the honour they do in
asking me. For it is an honour, and on a day such as this, one
of the greatest a very special friend can bestow upon one.

I certainly am aware of this and am tremendously grateful
for being asked. I will make a strange confession too:
Although anticipating making this little speech has for
weeks taken a great deal out of me, I would not have liked it
if someone else had been asked instead of me. That's life isn't
it?

And so, Ladies and Gentlemen, the honour of replying to
the bridesmaids toast is mine.

On their behalf I must say thank you very much to the
bridegroom for the kind, but, mark you, deserved
compliments he has paid them, and to all of you who have
gone out of your way to be sweet and kind to them.
They are very happy to be here as Jill's bridesmaids, and
want me to thank all of you for being so nice to them.

Ladies and Gentlemen, on behalf of my lovely charges,
thank you very much.

Best Man's Speech No. 5

Until Jack and Jill did me the signal honour of asking me to be their best man I could not understand this best man business at all.

Surely, I said to myself, the bridegroom is the best man – the bravest, the luckiest, most desired man.

Not his side-kick, the guy whose only job is to produce the wedding ring at the appropriate time so that the groom can pop it on the bride's third finger – left hand!

How wrong one can be! This is the voice of experience.

Just listen to me and maybe you will have second thoughts about who is the best man ...

First of all the best man must be a bachelor.

They dare not ask a married man. Married men are experienced, know what it is all about.

Bachelors know nothing of those mysteries which convert a miss into a missus or the endless preparations which go into managing this.

For the information of those who have not had the experience, let me tell you.

A best man is some kind of Boy Scout. You know, a chap brimming over with bonhomie, dedicated to good turns – that sort of man.

This paragon – yes, that is what I am ...! This paragon must be brave, have the kind of bravery that falters not when sorting out all kinds of intimidating people – from harrassed vergers to irate traffic wardens and including demanding dowagers or their ogre husbands.

He must make the path seem straight and even when really it is not a path at all but a burning deck with a cargo of hobgoblins.

He is the bridegroom's steadying influence, the cheerful chap who sees to everything, and keeps his head in all the emergencies.

Responsibilities – dear me, I'll tell you. Do you know I dared not even let myself go at last night's stag? There was so much to do this morning.

The best man is responsible for getting the groom to church on time. Yes, the best man has to help dress the groom. See to it that his pockets don't bulge with the usual paraphernalia.

And then I had to make sure that we had extra handkerchiefs – a vicar told me to see to that one.

Above all I had to make sure of the ring. All Jack did was keep asking about it. I nearly had a nervous breakdown checking again and again that it was actually in my pocket.

Had I taken it out, even once, I'm sure I'd have lost it.

You've no idea of what I went through before we got to the Church – the strain of it.

But all that disappeared miraculously in church – my worries melted away the moment our enchanting bride arrived with her wonderful retinue.

Beauty and light came in with the bride and her lovely bridesmaids.

Since their arrival all has been well, very well with me.

Feast your eyes upon them, ladies and gentlemen. They are charm itself. As soon as they appeared the scene changed, everything became sweetness and light, and I became the happiest of mortals. They are my good fairies. In their presence the hobgoblins dare not materialise.

And so, Ladies and Gentlemen it is, on their behalf, my great pleasure to thank Jack for the super way in which he proposed the toast of the bridesmaids who like me myself wish Jill and you everything that is best in the new life which you are now starting.

Best Man's Speech No. 6 (A brief one)

Actually when Jack asked me to make this speech I had the grace not even to pretend to say no. Instead, I said 'What must I say?'

He gave me one of his despairing looks then said 'I've got to propose the toast to the bridesmaids and you have to reply to it'.

I must have looked bewildered for he went on 'That means just say thank you'.

And I am very glad to do that ladies and gentlemen. Our charming bridesmaids are very grateful to you for the courteous way which all of you have treated them and for the many compliments you have paid them. Compliments for their beauty, taste, dress, decorum, indeed everything. They love you too. On behalf of these delightful, beautiful young ladies who have done so much to make this a red-letter day which will be remembered always by everyone here, thank you one and all very much.

2
Speeches For The
Bride's Father

The Bride's father is generally the first to speak, but sometimes he prefers to hand over this duty to another relative, or even a friend, who may be a more experienced speaker. The speeches which follow could (with adaptation) be suitable for a substitute speaker, but see also Chapter 4 page 49.

Bride's Father's Speech No. 1

It gives me great pleasure to wish Jack and Jill every happiness in their married life.

Today my wife and I formally welcomed Jack into our family as a son. Actually he assumed this role some time ago. Because we knew of Jill's feelings for him we were glad that he did so.

Jill and he didn't keep any of us too long in suspense once they decided they were really meant for each other.

They haven't been a bit like the couple I was told about when my wife and I were arranging today's wedding ceremonies.

This couple had been courting for nearly thirty years. Every evening during that time the man called on the woman at her comfortable home. She would make him a big supper and afterwards they would sit together before a lovely fire.

One evening, however, after supper, as they were sitting down looking into the fire, the woman said: 'John, don't you feel it's about time we started thinking about getting married?'

'Married!' exclaimed John. 'Good heavens, who will have us now?'

The other day I overheard a young man asking some friends whether married men live longer than bachelors. Before anyone else had a chance to reply a gloomy-looking man retorted: 'No, it only seems longer!'

My wife is here so I hastily add that he was quite wrong. Statistics prove that married men do live longer than bachelors ... honestly!

But maybe that gloomy-looking man had that morning quarrelled with his wife. That being so his outlook would be prejudiced.

Arguments between husbands and wives do take place, I'm afraid. And married people occasionally have differences. It is undoubtedly a very good thing to be prepared for such occasions at the beginning of marriage and have an arrangement to avoid quarrelling at such times.

I heard a healthy-looking man say at a wedding some time ago that he and his wife had such an arrangement. 'When a quarrel is starting,' he said, 'one of us immediately leaves the house.' He paused and added unexpectedly, 'That's why I look so well. I get plenty of fresh air!'

Undoubtedly, this man was attending that wedding without his wife! Not content with giving us the reason for his robust appearance he went on to say that he had been married for twenty years.

'When I married my wife,' he said, 'I thought she was an angel. And I still think so. I've got three reasons for this. Firstly, she's always up in the air. Secondly, she has never got anything to wear and lastly, she is always harping on something.'

You can all see that my wife is here! I don't call her an angel. I don't want her to fly away. I enjoy married life. I like my home comforts. At home I am a man of peace. After you've learned about marriage strategy, you'll find that's the safest way!

Jack, Jill, we wish you every happiness. Make up your minds to be happy, the two of you, and you will be happy.

Ladies and gentlemen, will you please stand up and drink a toast to the health, wealth and happiness of Jack and Jill?

Bride's Father's Speech No. 2

Everyone knows that very popular wedding hymn 'Love divine all loves excelling. Joy of Heaven to Earth come down.' And everyone here hopes and prays that this is how this marriage will be. Indeed we are confident it will be woven of pure unbounded love, freely given and joyfully received.

But I will not pretend that some people – cynics of course – feel that there ought always to be a second wedding hymn. It is however seldom sung at weddings, but with the gift of prophecy maybe often should.

That hymn?

'Fight the good fight with all thy might'.

I am very pleased to tell you that the one which will be appropriate for your married life depends little, if at all, on fate – it depends on you.

Yes, Jack and Jill, your marriage will be what you make it, I am glad to say.

We, your friends and relatives, have come here today to pray that it will be your paradise.

When Jack came to ask me for Jill's hand – oh yes, he very properly did that. He is really quite a splendid chap you know.

Anyhow, from that day I have been going around asking friends if they have any helpful words which I could pass on to them when I came to make my speech today.

Here are a few of those – er – topical tips which

incidentally have passed the – er – censor – who, as Jack already knows, is my better half.

The bonds of matrimony are not worth much if the interest is not kept up.

Man has his will but woman has her way.

Woman will be the last thing civilised by man.

Love is nature's second sun.

It is impossible to love and be wise.

Discreet wives have sometimes neither eyes nor ears.

Keep your eyes wide open before marriage and half-shut afterwards.

And finally, a little prayer should help the two of you.

"Please God, Give me the Serenity to accept the things I cannot change.

The courage to change the things I can

And the wisdom to know the difference."

Jack and Jill, may your love for one another, so evident for all to see today, continue all the days of your life, and may God bless you with health, wealth and happiness.

Ladies and Gentlemen I give you the toast of the bride and bridegroom.

Bride's Father's Speech No. 3

'Marriages are made in heaven', so goes an old proverb. We all hope that this is so and particularly that this one today is registered there.

This morning we witnessed a solemn ceremony in church in which our forefathers have participated and revered for hundreds of years.

And touchingly beautiful it was – the decorated Church, the moving words of the ritual, the marvellous music.

There, reverentially, before their God, Jack and Jill pledged themselves to one another for all time. These were moments of magic – of wonder – they were divine.

That was Part One of this wedding.

What I like to think of as Part Two is taking place here and now. This is the part at which their friends add their seal to the pledges made this morning in Church.

And when we part from here the marriage will truly have taken place before God and their fellow men. Long may it prosper.

It is during this second part of the ceremony that we the witnesses of this morning's dedication get to know one another, get to know better the friends and relatives of our new son and our daughter. Indeed those who are responsible for this get together – Jack and Jill – may themselves be meeting some of their new relatives for the first time. May they approve of one another. They will, I feel sure, do their best, remembering that first impressions are tremendously important in friendships. We will all do our best to create the atmosphere for it. We hope that the new friendships made today at this wedding between Jack's family and ours will create understanding and affection between our two families.

We welcome Jack into our family and we are glad to believe that his is doing the same to our beloved daughter.

No doubt as we get to know each other there will be a little adjusting to do on both sides.

The other day I heard about a Lord who had allowed the ground of his stately home to be used for a cricket match in connection with the village's Carnival week and even promised to take part in it. He himself was batting and his butler umpiring when suddenly there was a crack and the ball had hit his lordship's cricket pad.

'Howzat' shouted the bowler.

Boldly the umpire announced.

'His lordship is not at home'. His lordship looked aghast. 'What the devil do you mean by that?' he demanded. The umpire eyed him as only butlers can. 'I mean, milord, that you are out'.

There are bound to be little adjustments and changes to make in our two families but with a little goodwill on both sides I am certain they will be taken in our stride.

My toast, Ladies and Gentlemen, is that of the bride and bridegroom. God bless their marriage.

Bride's Father's Speech No. 4

> *Jack Sprat could eat no fat*
> *His wife could eat no lean*
> *So it came to pass between them both*
> *They lived together all serene.*

Which is not exactly how this verse of the old nursery rhyme actually ends, but my new last line makes it the best advice to newly-weds I can give.

An American poet put it rather better with

'A good husband makes a good wife'. My wife and I think we have made a good daughter. It's up to you Jack to make a good wife of her.

But it's up to the two of them to make it a good marriage. No one but your two selves can do that.

We, who have passed the learner stage, and had some time to look around, had time to consider that most fascinating Human Scene, will tell you that one of the great secrets of a happy marriage is Give and Take.

Yes, both.

And remember it is sometimes harder to learn to take.

Joan Sprat might at first, have quite liked fat, and possibly deliberately persuaded herself to go off it.

I've noticed that Jack and Jill have already learned something of this lesson. Jill is no longer as keen on some things as she was. And Jack, I'm told, was not always so much the stay-in bird that he has become during the past few months.

During those months my wife and I have got to know him pretty well. Obviously we approve of the young man we have got to know.

If we had not, I would not, in church, have handed him our Jill to care for until death do them part. Indeed, had my wife and I not really liked or approved of him I would not have been allowed to give him Jill this morning. That, Jack, is something you'll come to understand as the years go by. Remember man has his will but woman has her way. That is how love and understanding will sort it out and it will not be in the least painful.

But I must stop so that the two of you can start getting on with those things for yourselves. Jill is part of our love, experience and understanding, and now that I think of it it doesn't seem all that long ago since I was teaching her the very nursery rhyme about Jack and Joan Sprat with which I started.

Jack and Jill, may you be as happy as poets would have their lovers. My wife and I will always pray for this, and will do all in our power to make it so.

Ladies and Gentlemen, will you please rise to drink the most important toast of the day – The bride and bridegroom. God bless them both.

Bride's Father's Speech No. 5

Everybody called upon to make a speech, other than your professional spouters, says it! You may not hear the words, but the moment they stand up the words are those dominating the mind.

And I am saying it now, 'Good heavens, I wish someone else were doing this!'

But as the father of the bride I've no choice, it's a must. I must propose the main toast of the day. That of the Bride and Groom. God bless them both. Etiquette says it's the bride's father's privilege. Privilege? That's a misnomer if ever there was one. Huh! You should see my knees – perhaps you can hear them knocking, one against the other – to me as loud as castanets.

I wouldn't do this speech-thing for anyone other than our own dear daughter, whom today I gave away to Jack.

Oh, I must add her mother was very much in on it too! In on it all, from the very beginning. Before I even saw Jack properly.

You bachelors after you've joined the married state will soon learn that in matters concerning the family, the wife knows first and best. Yes, I said knows best! You must consult her. Moreover take her advice in these matters.

If you don't it all goes wrong somehow.

There, that's the first tip I've given you, Jack.

I won't give you any more just now but should you any time wish to listen to the Voice of Experience on matters helpful towards – er – matrimonial bliss, Wednesdays are always convenient. Eight o'clock. The wife's out then.

You are now in The Club – The Matrimonial Club, and I can tell you things about life and living you wouldn't understand until now.

You saw the initiation ceremony this morning. Once a man's gone through that, he's in. No matter what, Jack from now on you've got hundreds of willing listeners. Membership of the Club guarantees them. The only trouble is that most of them really want you to be the listener and when you are they do so go on! If you find they're too much, my advice to the two of you is get yourselves a dog. That'll do all the listening for you – and won't bark your secrets in the street next day, which too many humans just have to do!

One thing I beg of you both. Please, the two of you, don't think of us – your In-laws – as Out-laws. Indeed consider outlaws only those things which might make either of you unhappy.

Don't forget, Jack, a good wife and health are a man's best wealth.

And the most precious possession that ever comes to a man in this world is a woman's heart.

Jill has been a mother's pride and a father's joy.

And with a quote from Martin Luther made in 1569 I'll get

off my quaking legs.

'There is' Martin Luther wrote, 'No more lovely, friendly and charming relationship, communion or company than a good marriage'.

May yours, Jack and Jill, be such a one, is the wish of us all who now rise to drink to that.

Ladies and Gentlemen, I give you the toast of the day – Jack and Jill.

Bride's Father's Speech No. 6

After the solemnity of the marriage service and because we are all a little sad at losing Jack and Jill for a few days, I thought it might be a good idea to try to brighten things up with a few light-hearted remarks.

I am sure that it is because the wedding ceremony – the giving and taking of one another – is so charged with emotion that wedding receptions with follow-ups like this were invented. They are a sort of balance to what has gone on before. And I can tell you that a great deal of preparation went on before this wedding, which, because I myself was not as involved as some, I can proudly say was an Oscar winning performance.

As for me, my main role is to come. Actually it is the most unpleasant connected with the day – I have to pay!

Jill and her mother have for weeks been very much afraid that something might go wrong – because actually so much could, so they very wisely made a note of these on cards as they occurred to them.

By this morning all these cards except one had been dealt with. This last one Jill gave to me to keep until our car reached the church. Then she asked me for it.

As I handed it to her I noticed that there were three words on it.

These three words named in sequence the places we had to be at for the service. They were Aisle, Altar and Him.

All of you know the drill. Down the aisle to the altar to stand by him, the bridegroom.

Well, the moment we got inside church she started saying them like a Hindu Mantra.

Aisle, altar him;

Aisle, altar him

I'll alter him!

I'LL ALTER HIM

Marriage is, as everybody knows a lottery, but if you lose you just can't tear up the ticket and forget about it. Some say the prizes are all blanks. But today Jack has won himself a prize and Jill has by no means drawn a blank. She has got her man and man, according to a French moralist, is the reason why women don't love one another!

The two of them have from today increased the number of their relatives, for instance each now has a mother-in-law. And the two brand-new ones here today are splendid ladies, truly well-meaning, no matter what the comics say. And they do say some dreadfully unkind things. Actually though, one amused me the other day when he said that the heaviest penalty in law for bigamy was getting two mothers-in-law.

But from what I know of Jack and Jill bigamy is the last thing they are likely to think about – they are so full of one another. Everyone can see that they are terribly in love and idyllically happy.

This fact suddenly struck a young bride just as their taxi reached their honeymoon hotel:

'Jack,' she said 'Can't we pretend to be an old married couple'.

'How?' said he, actually wanting all the world to know... and be warned off.

There was one of those unhelpful pauses which went on so long that the taxi driver chipped in.

'You want to look an old married couple? O.K., Lady, I'll tell you. You carry the cases into the hotel'.

I do not imagine that Jack and Jill will be taking such precautions, but perhaps there are one or two that they should.

Two newly weds I heard about last week most certainly wished they had.

They were very modern and ... er ... shall we say in their own way, rather grand.

They had even fixed themselves with a new home at which, when they got back from their honeymoon, they gave a house-warming party.

One of the things they boasted about was that they had gone in for TWIN beds. And they made too much of a thing of talking about hygiene and such like matters, which almost everyone accepted with tongue-in-cheek.

But the evening was a great success and afterwards letters and phone calls came from everyone.

A week later the two were due to go back to work and so, the following morning, would have to get up early. For this they needed an alarm clock – but where was it?

Eventually, after much searching the bride had an idea. Her brother had given it to them as a house-warming present. Would he remember where she had put it?

After a while they managed to get him on the telephone. They beat about the bush a bit and came to the point when he was asking his sister whether her husband snored – that sort of thing with an added: 'How are you managing with the twin beds.' 'Splendidly they're great' she said, 'We both sleep like tops'. Then she added her $64,000 question, 'But we need to get up early tomorrow, and can't find the alarm clock you gave us'.

She could not understand why he laughed so uncontrollably until he got out, 'I put it in one of your twin beds'.

I'll finish with a quote from old Bill Shakespeare who always puts things much better than us.

'God the best maker of marriages, combine your hearts in one'.

Ladies and Gentlemen, I give you the toast of the day – the Bride and Groom – Bless them both.

3
Speeches For The Bridegroom

The Bridegroom is generally the second to speak. He should include in his speech thanks to the Bride's parents, thanks to the guests for their presents, and conclude with a toast to the bridesmaids. A short speech might go something like this:

Bridegroom's Speech No. 1

First of all I want to say thank you to all of you for coming to our wedding and joining us here afterwards. My wife and I are delighted to have you here enjoying yourselves with us on this the happiest day of our lives.

I want to say thank you too to everyone who has wished us good luck, health and happiness, particularly those who in doing so have undergone the ordeal of making a speech.

This seems to me to be an appropriate moment for me to thank my father and mother for being such splendid parents to me. I only hope that Jill and I make as good a job of our married life as they have of theirs. And ... er ... that all our children are as nice as I am!

Jill and I are very grateful to those kind people who have given us such excellent presents. Every time we look at them they bring joy to our hearts.

To our splendid best man, our greatest thanks. He has been our strength, a beacon in a sea of troubles.

Our special gratitude too, to our delightful bridesmaids, who have contributed so much to the beauty and excellence of this wonderful day.

It is their toast that I now have the privilege and delight to propose. Ladies and Gentlemen, our Bridesmaids.

Bridegroom's Speech No. 2

Today you witnessed a metamorphosis. It happened to Jill. From a Miss she metamorphosised to being a Missus. But Jill is not, as in the musical 'Cats' a cat – to call her kitten is permissible, but cat, no!

She is everything that is good, beautiful and wonderful and she is now my beloved wife – and, now, seemingly, also starting to look embarrassed ... !

Er ... Ladies and Gentlemen, my wife – there, that was the first time for me really to call her that! Ahem, my wife and I want to thank all of you for coming to share with us this our happiest day. And, particularly, I want to thank my new parents. Without them there would be no Jill and without Jill obviously none of us would be here enjoying this super occasion. Today, they have given Jill to me to love and cherish, and to that I will, henceforth, devote my life. We both thank them very much too for this delightful reception, which we are all enjoying immensely. There are other parents we both want to thank too – mine. They have been wonderful parents to me, and, today, I have partly repaid them by bringing them a new daughter who will, I assure them, be far less troublesome than I have been.

And who knows how long it will be before I will be bringing Jill and a newer-still member of the family to add to their happiness? Like Tiny Tim said, God bless us all.

Thank you, all of you too, for giving us such wonderful wedding presents. We do prize them and are most grateful to you. Bless you.

Jill and I also want to thank my – er – father-in-law. That's another new name I've collected today – Jill and I want to thank my father-in-law for the very nice way he has proposed our toast. Thank you, Dad.

And, lastly, we want to say a very, very big thank you to those marvellous young ladies who, next to my bride, are really the most beautiful in the room – our bridesmaids. They have been perfect and a tremendous help. And it is now my great pleasure to propose their very good health and happiness.

Ladies and Gentlemen, I give the toast to the bridesmaids.

Bridegroom's Speech No. 3

When I first met Jill . . . ! That was at a disco, and I remember thinking: 'She's nice, very nice . . .! !' But I certainly did not think that I would be here today thanking her father for proposing our health as the bride and bridegroom. Our love was not a sudden explosion. It is something which has grown with our tender care and of which neither of us is therefore likely to repent at leisure. We thank you very much father-in-law for the kind things you have said, and for so generously being the Founder of this Feast. Many thanks also to my father for doing so much for me. To our two mothers, too, thanks be for everything. We hope some day to prove that your bid for immortality has not been in vain, by perpetuating your genes into generations to come, or as the King James' version of the Bible so quaintly puts it – by multiplying.

And we want to thank those who made our union meet and right – the Vicar and all the staff of his beautiful church which so many of you attended.

Thank you, one and all, for coming here. We hope that you are enjoying yourselves and will continue to do so throughout the day.

You have given us wonderful wedding presents which we much appreciate – thank you so much.

Particularly, Jill wants me to thank the bridesmaids who,

she says, have been so kind and helpful to her. Not only today, but throughout the nervous weeks which went in preparation for today. I would like to add mine too, and say that they look just wonderful.

Already, I have noticed naughty twinkles in the eyes of some of the – er – swain, here present. Watch 'em girls. I'm pretty sure that the intentions of some of them are strictly dishonourable. Nevertheless, bear in mind that, play your cards right, and another enchanting day like this can be arranged very easily – to our mutual joy and happiness. So go to it all you eligibles. Wouldn't it be great if all the unmarried here today were, within twelve months, like us, married ... and blissfully happy?

Ladies and Gentlemen I give you the toast of these marvellous young ladies who are our bridesmaids.

The bridesmaids.

Bridegroom's Speech No. 4

If, as the worldly-wise say, marriage is a lottery then I am a winner and have got the first prize which has made me the happiest of men.

I am the luckiest, too, to have won Jill who will now have to get used to being called Mrs. Jack Smith. Sounds good, doesn't it? It gets all my bells ringing anyway!

And that is not the total of my good luck.

There are Jill's parents who are our generous hosts here today. Mine too, who have been such good parents to me. I am very lucky to have them. I could not have chosen better myself.

Then there are you – yes, all of you. You are not just a lucky dip among my acquaintances, but a treasure chest of those friends whom Jill and I regard as the priceless jewels of our lives.

Thank you, all of you, for coming, and for the splendid presents which you have given us.

And lastly – one keeps one's best thanks, like one's

goodies, until the end. Lastly, there are our adorable brides-maids. Today they are the most scintillating jewels in our treasure chest. They look lovely don't they? But, believe me, they are not mere decorations to this occasion. Jill says she does not know what she would have done without them – their help, advice and support. Not only today, but during the preparations in the weeks that have gone by.

It is now my great pleasure to propose their toast. Ladies and Gentlemen, I ask you to be up-standing and drink heartily to the toast of the bridesmaids.

Bridegroom's Speech No. 5

My wife and I ... That somehow doesn't sound right! Doesn't come trippingly on the tongue as Hamlet puts it, does it? And the reason why is not that I am a brand-new newly-wed. It is because we are all accustomed to 'My husband and I'.

I'll try again: My wife and I ... ah, well ...!! Anyhow, Jill and I want to thank you all for coming to our splicing, and for all the lovely presents you have given us.

Particularly, we want to thank Jill's parents for this splendid beano. You know, I cannot understand why they are so nice and kind to me, for in reality I am the thief who came and stole their daughter.

I do, however, promise them to do my best to be worthy of her, and to make her as happy as I can.

My parents? Well, I can never thank them properly for being so good to me.

It seems that today I have become a much more worthy person. I now have a better half, a help-mate, a consort, a spouse; and I myself am a Lord and Master. Phew!

Lord and Master? Well, there's no harm in kidding oneself, is there?

Even so, permit me to remind you of what one of the greatest sex symbols of our time, the actress Marilyn Monroe, had to say on this.

She said: 'I don't mind living in a man's world as long as I can be a woman in it.'

The film star Marilyn Monroe was herself a beauty, and there is a lot of that here today in addition to my bride, who alone surpasses that of our delightful bridesmaids whose toast I am about to propose.

We are very grateful to them for all the help they have given us so freely, and for being so charming to everyone, particularly our parents. Thank you very much all of you. You have made this a wonderful day.

And now, may I ask you please to raise your glasses and drink heartily the toast to the bridesmaids.

The bridesmaids.

Bridegroom's Speech No.6

This is the loveliest, the happiest, the most joyous day of my life.

Thank you all for helping to make it so – by coming! Lord Byron, who knew a thing or two about love, joy and happiness, put it rather well with his:

'All who joy would wish
Must share it – Happiness was born a twin
So pass this on. Make my happiest day yours too.'

Everyone has been most kind to Jill and me, and we thank you, all of you, but especially our parents for producing us, for rearing us, and for bringing us up to this our Happiest Day.

To all of you who are here and have given us such lovely presents, thank you. We will have such happy times when we return from our honeymoon talking about them, and about this day, to you, their donors.

During our honeymoon we'll send all of you cards ... we hope! If you don't receive them, don't be disappointed ... and don't really blame the post office. It's the thought that counts ... and you know about people in love; how it takes them away from reality, blissfully into wonderland which is where Jill and I will be, it's a place where people can't find time to write, no matter how they wish to tell their friends and relations how enchanting it all is. Think of us please as lovers in love and forgive our neglect.

We want to say thank you specially to our bridesmaids and my best man. Without them we would have been lost. They have certainly smoothed our path. Actually this toast is only to the bridesmaids.

What did Tennyson say about bridesmaids? Wasn't it: 'A happy bridesmaid makes a happy bride?' And Jill is happy, very happy, look at her.

I cannot find anything that the poets have said about the best man. And, between ourselves, although mine has performed his duties in the most exemplary manner he is the only one here complaining.

'Why', he asks, 'do the bridesmaids get a toast, but not me, the best man?'

He's got a point there, we must admit. And like I said, he has carried out his duties and looked after me in an exemplary fashion – a really splendid fellow.

Between ourselves – better than I expected. I anticipated at least one practical joke from him. Like, at the altar, when the organ was booming forth the wedding march and the bride's party was advancing upon us, a whisper in my ear: 'Jack, I can't find the ring, have you got it.' Imagine how I would have felt! Panic, did someone say? God, help me!

I am very lucky in that Jill likes him too, which means that he, like the bridesmaids will always be welcome at our home, which some sage has said is the wife's castle.

Actually, as I have said, this is the toast to the bridesmaids, but I would, if I may, like to couple with it one to our best man.

Ladies and Gentlemen will you please stand, raise your glasses and drink the toast to the bridesmaids and the best man?

4

Other Wedding Speeches

Speeches by Bride's Father, Bridegroom and Best Man are all that is usually required at weddings nowadays, but sometimes the Bride's Father is absent and/or prefers someone else to deputise, or else a fourth speech may be expected from someone representing the bridegroom's family. One of the following may be suitable:

Extra Speech No. 1

William Penn, years after he had added Pennsylvania to our empire wrote:

'Never marry but for love;
But see that thou lovest what is lovely.'

Both Jack and Jill have done that as we all can see, and today they are at their best.

They have not married in haste but have gone through, shall we say, the proper channels. They will not, therefore, according to the sages, repent at leisure.

In the 17th century the makers of proverbs were saying: 'Marry first and love will follow.'

Jack and Jill, there can be nothing but bliss in store for you, provided that you bear in mind another ancient proverb which tells us that:

'Marriage with peace is this world's paradise;
With strife, this life's purgatory.'

Remember what the poet William Cowper said: 'A disputable point is no man's land', and you'll always have peace. Emmerson gave another piece of helpful advice: 'Let a man behave in his own house as a guest.'

About the same time, another American observer of the human scene was very perceptively writing: 'Man has his will but woman has her way.'

A wife should always remember that a man is happy to be King or peasant who finds peace in his home.

Jack and Jill, now that you are both prisoners of wedlock and about to set up your own home, I hope you'll find what others have said about that helpful.

Let's start with Cervantes:

'You are a King by your own fireside, as much as any monarch on his throne.'

Kipling in his 'Our Lady of the Snows' gives us the experience of one lady:

'Daughter am I in my mother's house, but mistress in my own.'

A more contemporary author has observed perceptively:

'A man's home is his wife's castle.'

And finally there is Emmerson again:

'The ornament of a house is the friends who frequent it.'

To the two of you, Jack and Jill, I would wish the serenity to accept the things you cannot change; the courage to change the things you can; and the wisdom to know the difference.

May God bless the two of you and give you health, wealth and happiness all the days of your life.

Extra Speech No. 2 (Honeymoon)

In a little while Jack and Jill will be leaving us to go on their honeymoon which I am told is also sometimes called 'honey-month'. Traditionally it lasted a whole month and was commonly spent in travelling before settling down to the business of life.

May their honeymoon be the best, most enjoyable holiday of their lives.

Here, maybe, I should, however, strike a cautionary note and tell them about the newly-weds who went to the seaside for their honeymoon.

On being shown the door of their room in the hotel, the young husband gallantly picked up his bride and carried her across the threshold.

A week later when they were leaving she supported him to the lift and carried him out to their waiting taxi.

But love seems to have addled the minds of that couple for when they first entered their hotel bedroom she uttered a little cry of dismay as she saw that there were twin beds.

'What's the matter, darling?' he asked anxiously.

Already there was a tear in her eye and she answered with a catch in her voice: 'Darling, you told me we were going to have a room to ourselves!'

The following morning he took her to the beach and as they watched the waves he began to quote Byron:

'Roll on, thou dark and deep blue ocean, roll!'

'Darling', she interrupted him. 'Oh, you are wonderful. Look, it's doing it!'

The season was not yet properly started and their small hotel was having some difficulty in recruiting staff so the service was not all that it could be.

On their first evening they decided to have their baths before dinner. He went to the bathroom at the end of the corridor and she to the one almost next door to their bedroom, saying that it would take her much longer than him, and that she would see him later for a pre-prandial drink in the cocktail bar.

He had had several drinks when she arrived, almost two hours later.

He looked at his watch, 'Darling' he expostulated 'surely you don't take two hours for a bath?'

Tears welled up in her eyes. 'There was no curtain in the bathroom', she sobbed 'and I had to keep getting out to breathe on the window.'

Before the end of the week her mother sent them their local paper in which there was an account of their wedding. Mother-in-law had underlined the last few words of that and added a note which read: 'I'm sure he deserved it.'

The last few words of the paper's wedding report were: 'The gift of the bride to the bridegroom was a beautiful dressing-down.'

I began with a word of caution and now so to balance these few words, my last words are of caution too:

'Always remember that the critical period in matrimony is breakfast time, and too that any mud thrown is ground lost.'

I know that you are much more with-it than the cóuple I have been telling you about. Their experiences will not be yours, but it's never a bad thing to say to oneself: 'There but for the grace of God go I.'

And may God go with you not only on your honeymoon but all the days of your life.

Bless you both.

Extra Speech No. 3

Because, at weddings, it is the men who usually make the speeches most of these have been written from a man's point of view, and frequently poke good-natured fun at the ladies. The one which follows is different. It is one which is very much for the ladies. It should be delivered in friendly tones and in a not-too-serious manner, preferably by someone devoted to the Women's Liberation Movement.

If one of the male guests makes it he could exonerate himself by beginning with:

'Jill's mother feels that nowadays there is always too much pandering to the bridegroom's sex – our sex! – at weddings, and insisted that someone should favour the ladies with kind supportive words. Because I am already a member of the family I have been elected to do so. (OR: Because I am married and I have, by my wife, here present, been elected to do so!)'

Ladies and Gentlemen,

Today, Jack, in getting Jill to marry you, you have done inordinately well for yourself.

Let me quote for you what that renowned Victorian novelist Charles Reade had to say about a wife:

'A wife is essential to great longevity: She is the receptacle of half a man's cares and two-thirds of his ill-humour.'

An Irish Bishop named Jeremy Taylor, centuries earlier, wrote:

'A married man falling into misfortune is more apt to retrieve his situation in the world than a single one, chiefly because his spirits are soothed and retrieved by domestic endearments, and his self-respect kept alive by finding that although all abroad be darkness and humiliation, yet there is a little world of love over which he is monarch.'

Ladies and Gentlemen, take notice particularly. Those are not the words of two women's libbers; indeed their authors had been mouldering in their graves decades before those greatest of women, the suffragettes, were making their heroic stand.

Go further back still to the days when the Chinese were making proverbs for the world.

'A hundred men', says one of those, 'may make an encampment, but it takes a woman to make a home.'

Now, what would you say was the sex of the person who said:

'If a woman can be a sweetheart, valet, audience, cook and nurse, she is qualified for marriage?' Don't bother to answer – it's obvious! But isn't it also too true?

As we were standing outside the church this morning, watching Jack and Jill being photographed, a passer-by stopped to look, and asked me: 'Do you think she'll make him a good wife?'

'She will', I said. And I can bet you, all of you, here

present, what else she'll make him too . . . she'll make HIM A GOOD HUSBAND!

Far too frequently imputations are made regarding the Fair Sex without even the slightest justification. They hurt, you know.

Remarks like saying the Fair Sex should be called the UNfair Sex.

Or trotting out dubious definitions, such as:

'A bachelor is often a man who has been crossed in love; but a married man is one who has been double-crossed.'

Then there is that mischievous practice of relating snide stories like the one in which the foreman asks the new shop steward:

'Did my wife speak at this morning's staff meeting?'

To which the shop steward replies: 'I don't know your wife, Foreman. But a tall, fair lady did get up and say that she couldn't find words to express her feelings, and . . .'

There, the Foreman cuts him short. 'Couldn't find words to express her feelings', did you say? 'That certainly wasn't my wife!'

Here's another, a similar humbug.

In this the wife is made to say: 'I think married men should wear something to show they're married.'

That goads her miserable, little husband to protest: 'I do wear something which shows that I am married – this shiny suit!'

A more realistic picture of the domestic scene is conjured up by tales similar to the one about the poor wife who is wakened at night by noises downstairs. Scared, she turns to her husband who is at her side and whispers: 'I think that there are burglars downstairs. Are you awake?'

Stiff with fright, he says: 'No!'

Or there is this typical illustration of the way so many wives are treated.

'John, I can't stand much more of this. You don't consider me at all. I'm sick and tired of your carrying on as though I weren't here. You've been out at work all day and I've been here, on my own, with no-one to talk to. And now that you are home, you just sit there reading your old paper taking no notice at all of me ...! You don't love me any more ... that's it, isn't it?'

And her Lord and Master stirs himself to say: 'Darling, that's utter nonsense. Every time you come near me you turn me on. Every day, I love you more and more. Honestly, I worship the ground on which you walk. Your every wish is my command ...!! But, for Pete's sake, let me get on with reading my horoscope!'

To you who are already married, I offer this piece of advice, take it or leave it, but I urge you to take it.

Try praising your wife ... even if, at first, it frightens her!

I started with words written by a one-time Bishop of Down and Connor and will end with another quote from him:

'A good wife is heaven's best gift to men – his gem of many virtues, his casket of jewels. Her voice is sweet music, her smiles his brightest day, her kiss the guardian of his innocence, her arms the pale of his safety, her industry his surest health, her economy his safest steward, her lips his faithful counsellors, her bosom the safest pillow of his cares.'

To you, Jack and Jill, our very best wishes.

Soon, you will be safely off on to your honeymoon; may it be all for which you hope, and splendid in every way.

As for me – poor me! Well, after my little speech: Is there, please, here, some kind Amazon who will escort me to the sanctuary of her hearth, where I will be safe from vengeful chauvinists for the rest of the day?

Extra Speech No. 4 (A sailor's viewpoint)

We have been to church and afterwards listened to worthy speeches, all of which have been excellent – far better than I am capable of delivering. In bed, last night, I was considering all this, and got to thinking that by the time my turn came, Jack and Jill and the rest of us might be a little tired of solemnity, and it might therefore be a good plan to turn aside for a short while from the serious, and tell you something about my Uncle Bill. My Uncle Bill is a sailor – okay, you have never heard of him. That's because we don't talk about him outside the family. The distaff side doesn't approve of him. He's the nearest we've got to a skeleton in the cupboard.

To begin with I don't think that he is actually married – but you know what sailors are.

Of his sailor friends Uncle Bill sings:

'We joined the Navy to sea the world

And what did we see

We saw the sea!'

Between ports, according to him, it's all routine and often just sheer boredom. Too much time for thinking, too much time for talking ... and too little to think or talk about.

And they only see the distaff side of humanity when they are in port. Deprived; he says they can think of little else. Their talk and thoughts are mostly: girls ... girls ... girls.

As to the question of holy matrimony, everyone knows that in this sailors are gentlemen of considerable experience – for has not a sailor a wife in every port?

Anyway, I thought you might be interested to hear some of the things my naughty Uncle Bill divulged to me.

Oh, Jack and Jill, don't take him too seriously. Remember what sailors are. 'Tell it to the marines' I dare say originated in the fo'castle, as the crew howled down a really tall story. Naïve marines on their first voyage would swallow anything, and like ships apprentices frequently did – the anchor.

One of the stories he relates is about two sailors who had not met for years but now were on the same ship again.

'Jack' said one, to his old friend who was now the ship's cook, 'Tell me did you marry that blonde in Liverpool you were so mad about ... or do you still darn your own socks and do your own washing?'

Jack's face fell. 'Yes', he said gloomily 'And I still do.'

The best advice for newly-wedded husbands, according to my Uncle Bill, is to act dumb and tell 'em nowt.

Presently Sailor Jack went on to boast about the accomplishments of his blonde wife from Scouse country. 'She can swim, ride, run, drive a car, and, next week, is going to learn to glide', he boasted. 'Really, she's a great all-rounder.'

His friend Tom sniffed and said: 'Then you must get along fine together. With all those things to do, the cooking will obviously be all yours!'

The two friends chatted on and presently Jack asked: 'Any good shows on in port?'

Tom thought a moment then said: 'There's a hypnotist on at the Alhambra. He hypnotised Jimmy-the-One on Tuesday.'

'What do you mean?' asked Jack. 'Hypnotised – what's that?'

'It means getting a man in your power and making him do anything you want.'

'That's not hypnotism', retorted Jack, 'that's marriage.'

They talked on, reminiscing as old friends do until presently Jack had the feeling that Tom was giving nothing away whilst he was telling all.

And so he turned to Tom and said: 'Tell me, how is it that you never got spliced yourself?'

Tom shrugged. 'Well, it's like this. When I was very young I promised my mother – God rest her soul – that I'd never marry until I found the ideal woman. Believe me, I sailed the seven seas before I found her.'

'Oh?' Jack's eyes became saucers. 'And then what?'

'Huh!' Tom's face fell. 'She was looking for the ideal man.'

You have found your ideal man, Jill, and you your ideal woman, Jack. Bless you both.

Take no notice of the silly stories I've told, instead remember:

'Grave authors say witty poets sing
That honest wedlock is a glorious thing.'

Extra Speech No. 5 (A Friend of the Bride's Family)

I was at a wedding a little while ago and heard a man who had been married a long time remark: 'Marriage is what you make it.'

I am sure that this is quite true, but when I tried giving this as a piece of advice to a friend he retorted: 'Yes, it does make two of you one, but it's a life-long struggle to discover which is that one.'

Even so, the famous Dr. Johnson declared as was his fashion: 'Marriage has many pains, but celibacy has no pleasures.'

A young lady who was sitting next to me at the wedding about which I spoke a moment ago said that she had asked her aunt, if during the many years of her married life, she had not thought of divorce. 'No,' said her aunt, 'only murder!'

The same young lady went on to say that marriage is popular with men because it combines the maximum of temptation with the maximum of opportunity.

But when she added the crack: 'A good wife laughs at her husband's jokes, not because they are clever, but because she is,' I thought it high time that I asked a male friend or two what they thought. I am glad to say that they were equal to the occasion and retorted with pungency.

Here are a few of their remarks:

'A man is incomplete until he's married and then he's completely finished.'

'Marriage is like a steaming bath. Once you're in it it's not so hot.'

'Marriage is the difference between painting the town and painting the back porch.'

A very happy looking man remarked: 'I've got the finest wife in the country–I hope she stays there!'

Well, as none of these points of view was really encouraging I decided to extend my inquiries. This time I asked more experienced, more stable people what they thought. This is what they had to say:

'A good marriage is like a good handshake – there is no upper hand.'

'Marriage resembles a pair of shears joined together so that they cannot be separated. Often they move in opposite directions. But woe betide anyone who comes between them.'

'A good wife is like the ivy which beautifies the building to which it clings, twining its tendrils more lovingly as time converts the ancient edifice into a ruin.'

Personally, I think that marriage consists not in two people looking into each other's eyes but in two people standing shoulder to shoulder, both looking in the same direction, bravely facing whatever life may put in their path.

I am sure that Jack and Jill will do this.

We all wish them every happiness, health, wealth and good luck.

Ladies and gentlemen I give the toast of the bride and bridegroom.

Extra Speech No. 6 (The Bridegroom's Father)

'By their fruits ye shall know them,' is a verse which I often heard quoted at school. Years have passed since those days. During them I have come to realize what a depth of truth that line contains. But it was only the other day that someone quoted me for its corollary. He was telling me about two schoolboy brothers who had broken his window. 'Ah,' he said, 'by their parents ye shall know them!'

It will be through Jill, what Jill really is, that we shall really get to know Bill and Anne Smith, just as they will really get to know my wife and myself through Jack.

We are very glad to be here today. Parents, you know, spend half their time worrying how their children will turn out and the other half wondering when they will turn in. From now on we will know where Jack is turning in!

We thank Bill and Anne for giving him the hand of Jill in

marriage and look forward to the day when it bears fruit. Babies not only make two families one; they are also the rivets which keep together the bonds of matrimony.

We welcome Jill into our family. We feel that we are not losing a son but gaining a daughter.

Her parents' happiness is bound to affect Jill so I ask you to be upstanding and drink to the health and happiness of the bride's parents.

5
An Engagement Party Speech

Engagement parties, by and large, are far too carefree for formalities. If you are called upon to make a speech the one which follows will be quite sufficient.

At engagement parties people don't want to listen to speeches. They prefer to enjoy themselves in other, more animated ways.

Speech

We are this evening celebrating the fact that Jack has given Jill an engagement ring. We congratulate the two of them and wish them every joy and happiness.

No one can say that Jill is a gold-digger. She has not 'broken' her 'date' by going out with him. Indeed she has done quite the contrary. By becoming engaged to Jack she has made him one of the 'landed' gentry.

Thank you for asking us to join you tonight. We are grateful to you for your friendship which will, we trust, live on, come what may.

A cynic said to me the other day that an engagement was the time a girl takes to find out if she can do any better.

This is quite untrue of Jill. She is looking forward with eagerness to the day when Jack gives her another ring – a wedding ring. We hope to be around then, to bless them both and wish them good luck.

And we hope to be around shortly after that when Jack buys yet another ring. Again, we will bless and congratulate them.

That third ring? What will it be? Why a teething ring, of course!

I give you the toast of Jack and Jill. May God be good to them and grant them health and happiness.

6
A Stag Party

Stag-parties! The double-barrelled name puzzled me to the extent that I consulted the dictionary. That answered with: 'Stag-dance-party: A dance or party of men only', and gave STIGAI as the Icelandic origin of the root, meaning to 'mount', which, I suppose, is fair enough, but what would the bridegroom's friends say if he invited them to the stag-dance of the dictionary? Should there still be a wedding in the offing?

Stag-parties are the most flexible of all the occasions concerned with a wedding, but, nonetheless, they can be tricky affairs. Guests should be particularly careful of what they say about the bride-to-be. Under no circumstances should anyone be allowed to besmirch her name in any way, no matter how tight they get.

Silly remarks about the bride-to-be's virtue or anatomy should never be made. Many a marriage has been ruined before it started because of some stupid remark made about the bride-to-be at a stag-party.

Some stag-parties are simply men-only dinner parties with speeches of which what follows is an example. It should be delivered in a light-hearted manner until almost the end.

Speech No. 1

This is almost the last night Jack will be a bachelor. What

possessed him to become engaged I do not know! But how Jill has stuck him this far is also beyond me.

Maybe they've heard that two can live as cheaply as one. Well, Christmas is about the only time when this is true. Married people have an advantage then – the two can give as cheaply as one. For the rest of the year the theory that two can live as cheaply as one is nonsense.

Jack perhaps doubts this. If he does, I suggest that on his honeymoon he takes a 50p bus ride. He'll find it will cost him a pound.

There is one piece of advice I want to give him tonight. It is that he makes the best of his honeymoon. It will be his last vacation before taking on a new boss.

Don't think I've got anything against Jill. I think she's a fine girl, and no doubt she will make Jack a wonderful wife. But marriage won't be so wonderful for her either; she's exchanging the attention of all the men she knows for the inattention of Jack.

I hope that Jack is satisfied with Jill's conversation now, and that he will continue to be satisfied with it until his old age, for I'm told that everything else in marriage is transitory.

Marriage, however, has one definite advantage; Jack won't ever again make a fool of himself without being told about it!

Perhaps Jack is tired of his bachelor life – just one undarned thing after another.

But I'm afraid that nothing short of a miracle will save him now. And you don't hear about many miracles being performed these days, do you? Indeed some people have difficulty in understanding what they are even. One of these was an Irishman named Patrick whose priest had spent a long time trying to explain to him what one was. Patrick, however, was still not satisfied. 'Could Your Reverence', he asked, 'please give me an example of a miracle?'

The priest thought for a moment then said: 'Yes, Patrick. Turn round, will you?'

Patrick turned round and as he did so the priest aimed a fearful kick at his behind. 'Did you feel that?' he asked.

'Sure, I did!' snarled Patrick.

'Well', said the priest, 'it would have been a miracle if you hadn't.'

Poor old Jack, I've kicked him pretty hard tonight. My conscience is at last starting to trouble me. I confess that I kicked him from purely selfish motives. You see, I'm afraid that when he marries I won't be seeing as much of him as I have in the past; that his domestic bliss will be domestic detention, and that for some considerable time ahead we will have to enjoy ourselves without him.

I wish him the best of good luck. May his marriage be a wonderful success. I ask you to drink to that.

At other stag-parties entertainment is provided, sometimes by professionals, sometimes by friends who do a turn, and sometimes by both.

In every case you must appoint a chairman and you should do this weeks in advance of the event. It is a good plan to ask your best man to be the chairman, except when you have a friend who has experience in organising such entertainment. He will know whom to ask for items for your programme, and a programme you must have. It is imperative that you arrange this in close collaboration with your chairman.

The entertainers should be seen days before your stag-party so that your chairman will know exactly what to expect of them, and they what they may count on from him. If these are amateur entertainers then the chairman would be very wise to let them know what time has been allocated to each item. I find that a limit of seven minutes is about right. Audiences are ready for a change after seven minutes and get restless. Many evenings have been marred by one artiste falling in love with the mike – and hogging it!

Should an item take less than seven minutes – well and good, for should he have come across very well, he can then be asked to give a second item later in the programme; a possibility of which the chairman should warn the artistes when he tells them that there is a seven minutes limit on all the items.

The concert party may have its own compère. If it has, the chairman should let him take over as soon as he has introduced it with a very short speech such as:

Speech No. 2 (Introduction of Artistes)

Gentlemen:

During the Victorian era children were told they should be seen and not heard, and that, once I've introduced our splendid entertainers, whom I know you are going to enjoy immensely, will be my role.

But before I sit down may I say that I have arranged that between items there will be suitable breaks for you to order drinks. This will give our friends the quiet they deserve. Please give it to them.

Gentlemen, it gives me great pleasure to present to you The Staggering Stag Show.

At the end of the show the chairman should use:

Speech No. 3

Gentlemen:

Before we go our various ways, I am sure you would wish me to thank our good friends for the excellent entertainment they have given us this evening. Your loud and frequent applause has been very convincing evidence of your enjoyment and appreciation. Thank you very much, Gentlemen, for such splendid fare for which my friends and I now, once again, show our appreciation ... applause!

The other kind of stag-party is by far the most frequent. For this the stags gather at some hostelry at which arrangements for some privacy have been made with the landlord ... and much drinking is done.

Again, it is wise to appoint a chairman, and for this I again recommend the best man. At such functions the best, fairest and most agreeable plan is to have a kitty, and guests should be given an estimate of what this might cost them before they come. At the party the chairman will be the toast-master and could set the ball rolling with:

Speech No. 4

Gentlemen:

Now that your glasses are charged, let us start formally by drinking to the health and happiness of Jack. God bless the old rascal and his bride-to-be. God Bless her too.

Well, that's the end of the formalities, and we can start on the stories.

Soon Jack is to have a mother-in-law. A mother-in-law is a formidable animal, and many a man would love to be in the boots of the young gentleman who, while driving his wife to the shops, was involved in an accident in which, unfortunately, her face got severely injured, and was afterwards very badly scarred.

In due course, they found a plastic surgeon who guaranteed he could do a skin graft which would restore her to her former beauty. There were, however, snags: It would cost them £500 and he would have to take the skin for the graft from the husband's behind.

They readily agreed to this, and a few months later the young wife was as beautiful as nature intended her to be, so her grateful happy husband put his money in an envelope and took it to the plastic surgeon, smiling all over his face.

The plastic surgeon opened the envelope, counted the

money and said: 'You've made a mistake, haven't you? My fee was £500 – there are six hundred here.'

'Oh no I haven't', said the husband 'the extra money is for the pleasure I get every time my mother-in-law embraces my wife and kisses my behind.'

Whilst you are thinking of one to cap that I'll give you another. This one is about friends, like us.

There was a man who arrived in the pub and he was leading a snake on a string.

The Landlord didn't like this at all but civilly enough asked: 'Is that snake poisonous?'

'Yes', said the customer.

'Well, if he bites someone, what happens then?'

'No bother, you just get a friend to suck the poison out of the wound.'

'Supposing', said the Landlord, 'that he bites my behind?'

'Then you'll get to know who your real friends are, won't you?'

And so on, ad infinitum ...!

7
A Silver Wedding

At a silver wedding celebration the husband and wife are still sufficiently young for fun. The speech which follows is a mixture of the light-hearted and the serious. It should suit the occasion ideally.

The Speech

There are many stories about marriage. The vast majority of them skit at it as an arrangement heavily loaded in favour of women. You know the sort of thing:

'A good husband is one who will wash-up when asked and dry up when told.'

'In marriage, it only takes one to create an argument – your wife!'

'Every time you argue with your wife words flail you.'

'Marriage is a bargain .. Er ... someone gets the worse of every bargain!'

If anyone wonders whether such remarks are true I suggest that they should come to a party such as this.

Any couple who have been married twenty-five years will tell you that the secret of being happily married is to be as polite and considerate to one another as you are to your best friends. The word to use above all others in your relationship together is 'ours'.

John and Mary Smith whose silver-wedding we are

tonight celebrating will I am sure endorse this.

Twenty-five years is a long period of time. If it were possible to confront John and Mary with themselves as they were twenty-five years ago, would they, I wonder, recognize each other? Physically, they doubtlessly would. But I venture to suggest that their personalities have changed unbelievably. Each has taken something from the other. Each has given something to the other. They have become almost as one. And each no doubt has improved as a result.

We congratulate them on reaching their silver wedding. That is no small achievement in this day and age. We look forward to the day when they will be celebrating their golden wedding.

And now, the toast: Health and many years of happiness to John and Mary Smith.'

8
A Golden Wedding

At a golden wedding everybody can be as sentimental as they like. There may be present children, grand-children and perhaps great-grand-children of the couple who are celebrating their golden wedding.

The speech which follows should be just right for the occasion.

The Speech

Today, we are celebrating an event which is becoming rarer and rarer in society. Fifty years of Married Life is no small achievement. Indeed, fifty years at any job is, these days, a record. And marriage is a job, which has to be worked at, as those who try it soon learn. John and Mary Smith have worked so well at it, giving and taking, loving and being loved, that they have become parts of an indivisible whole.

Fifty years ago John and Mary were young people, full of fun and vigour, laughing at the prospect of married life. I wonder what sort of jokes people were making about marriage in the days when John and Mary became part of that holy estate.

'The chain of wedlock is so heavy that it takes two to carry it?'

'In every home there are two ingredients for the perfect murder – a husband and a wife?'

'Why keep another man's daughter?'

'Yawning is a device of nature to enable husbands to open their mouths?'

I suppose the jokes were really pretty much then what they are now.

In fifty years of married life John and Mary will have heard them all, will have repeated them to one another and will have laughed at them together.

The other day I overheard a man being asked what he would like to be if there were such a thing as reincarnation and he returned to earth after death. 'Oh,' he said promptly, 'I'd like to be my wife's second husband.'

I'm sure that would be the ambition of John and Mary too if they ever had a second span of life.

John and Mary must be very proud of one another today. Their family must be delighted with them. Already I am sure the reminiscences are being exchanged. This is an occasion for sentiment and congratulations.

I feel honoured that the privilege of proposing a toast to two such charming people as John and Mary has been bestowed upon me.

May God spare them for many more years to be a joy to their family, friends and neighbours.

Ladies and gentlemen, will you please join me in drinking a toast to John and Mary. God bless them both.

9
A Christening

Christening parties are not occasions for stylized speeches. They are intimate occasions at which one might be called upon to say a few words. What follows should be ample.

I have made the imaginary baby a boy and given him the names of John Paul.

The Speech

The other day a little boy was quizzing his mother. 'You say the stork brings babies?' he asked.

'Yes,' answered his mother.

'And the Lord gives us our daily bread?'

'Yes, dear!'

'And Santa Claus brings us presents?'

'Yes ...!'

'Well, then,' the little boy frowned, 'why do we have to have Daddy?'

I could tell that little boy why we have to have a Daddy. We have to have one to attend parties such as this! Without a Daddy here this party would scarcely be proper!

No matter what that little boy felt we are glad to have this Daddy around. We congratulate both Jill and him on their lovely baby. I am sure that he will bring them great joy and happiness. In him they will live on.

Someone has said that a baby is an alimentary canal with a

loud voice at one end and no responsibility at the other.

Jack and Jill quite agree that both ends must function, but how they wish that the times at which they did were more convenient!

We wish this wonder of theirs whom we heard today christened John Paul every blessing.

We wish him health. We wish him wealth.
We wish him gold in store.
We wish him heaven when he goes.
Who could wish him more?

10
Eighteen Today

An eighteenth birthday party is an occasion for fun, not long speeches.

Frequently someone presents the lucky person whose birthday it is with a golden key. If there is to be but one speech at the party, then the key should be presented at its end. If you use the speech given below you should then alter the last paragraph to read: 'In presenting him with this golden key we wish him health, wealth and happiness. May he *live* all the days of his life.'

Speech No. 1

Ladies & Gentlemen,

'Old age is honourable.' That is a remark we sometimes hear. But the most wonderful age of all must be eighteen. It is the one birthday we all look forward to. The birthday we acknowledge. Later on some people like to have their birthdays remembered but not their ages.

Men sometimes take a day off for their birthday. Women, however, are often accused of taking off at least a year. This is really rather foolish for all you have to do to find any woman's age is ask her sister-in-law!

The other day I heard about a woman being subpoenaed to give evidence. Before she started the Clerk of the Court explained to her that she was only to speak of what she saw, smelt or did. She must not give hearsay evidence; that is, she must not speak of what she was told unless it was told to her by, or in the presence of, the accused. The Clerk then nodded to the prosecuting solicitor to begin.

'Madam,' began that worthy, 'what is your age?'

She stared at him a moment then smiled blandly before answering: 'I am not allowed to give hearsay evidence.'

But Gareth has not got to take hearsay evidence of his birthday. There are plenty around who remember it, chief of whom are, of course, his mother and father. They must both be particularly proud today. Proud because from now on there is another in their family who enjoys all the privileges of full citizenship in this our native land.

We congratulate them and we congratulate Gareth too.

We wish him health, wealth and happiness. May he have them all the days of his life.

Speech No. 2

You know that I can't make a speech. It's not me at all! But this little verse says all that I want to say:
 'Birthdays are like stepping stones
  Along the path of years;
 Here's hoping you will always find,
  As each new one appears
 That it's a stepping stone as well
  To joys and pleasures new,
 To still more happy hopes fulfilled,
  And still more dreams come true.'

Let's drink to that.

PART III

11
Introducing the Speaker

Introducing the speaker means that and no more. You should give your audience a brief synopsis of his career, qualifications and achievements, emphasizing his importance in relation to your organization, or audience.

This speech has been adapted from one I used when introducing our Member of Parliament before he made a speech at a civic dinner.

The next person I shall ask to speak is the gentleman who represents us at the Palace of Westminster. There he helps to make our laws. He is our representative there – yours and mine, no matter how we voted at the last general election.

My hope, and his, is that we did vote – each of us. We owe that to the past – to all those who lived their lives, and even sacrificed them so that we might have this vote in the government of our land.

Actually, I am a little sorry for him for he is seldom able to do full justice to any public dinner. You see, he is always haunted by the knowledge that he might be called upon to make a speech. This is, I suppose, what is known as an occupational hazard.

Having been Chairman of this Council for twelve months I have some idea of what this does to his enjoyment of an evening, and sympathize deeply with him.

But even so, I can't let him off. It would be wrong of me to do so. And most of you would rightly find fault with me.

Well, he really needs no introduction from me. You must all know him at least by sight. Some of you will have consulted him and enlisted his aid at one of those very helpful surgeries he holds on most Saturday mornings.

He is always a willing listener to everything that we have to say and ever a tireless worker on our behalf.

It gives me great pleasure to call upon our Member of Parliament (name) to address you.

12
Speeches of Welcome

When you deliver a welcome speech try to look happy.

After reading the following speeches you should have no difficulty in producing one when you have to welcome people.

Speech No. 1

I wonder if anyone here actually knows what my job is here this evening. I am here in three rôles. Firstly, I am Chairman of the Council. Secondly, I am here as your President, and thirdly I am here as Temporary, Acting, Unpaid Chairman of the Local Association, known to all boy scouts as the Local Ass.

My job this evening is to welcome you one and all. I hope that you will all have an excellent time with no embarrassing moments.

Recently, a certain County Council gave a dinner in honour of a newly-appointed officer. For the sake of anonymity we will call him Mr. Smith-Jones. Now we in Anglesey sent a representative to this function. Unfortunately, he had never clapped eyes on Mr. Smith-Jones. When he did, he turned to the strange lady who sat on his right and said: 'If that is Mr. Smith-Jones, I'm terribly disappointed. I expected him to be far more imposing and intelligent-looking.'

The lady stiffened. 'I beg your pardon,' she said. 'That is Mr. Smith-Jones ... And do you know who I am?'

Our man shook his head.

'I am Mrs. Smith-Jones.'

For a moment or two our man was dumbstruck but presently he recovered himself sufficiently to ask: 'Do you know who I am?'

'I do not,' she answered haughtily.

'Well, thank God for that,' said he getting up to leave.

But his experience was not half so bad as that of a young lady who because she had a touch of hay-fever took two handkerchiefs with her to a dinner party, one of which she tucked in her bosom.

At dinner she began rummaging to the right and to the left in her bosom for the fresh handkerchief. Engrossed in her search she suddenly realized that conversation had ceased and people were watching her, fascinated. In confusion she murmured: 'I know I had two when I came in.'

A frequent cause of embarrassment at dinner parties is the practice of calling upon someone for a speech without giving him previous warning. That man's plight is often the same as that of the mosquito who arrived at a nudist camp, surveyed the territory and said, 'I don't know where to begin.'

Actually every man who has to make a speech has my sympathy for accustomed as I am to public speaking I know the futility of it.

During my year of office I have had the pleasure of boring many an audience. I've always ignored that doubtlessly excellent advice to all *other* speakers: 'If you don't strike oil in the first three minutes, stop boring.'

Mind you, there have been two or three impolite characters who have objected. This is how they did so:

'You know, old man, almost every after-dinner speech has a happy ending – everyone is glad when it's over.'

'Er ...! Good speeches are like pie. They're better with plenty of shortening.'

'Dear boy, I always think a speech is like a bad tooth – the longer it takes to draw it out, the more it hurts.'

Of course, during my year of office I have had to listen to several speeches too.

One thing soon became evident. The jawbone of an ass is just as dangerous today as in the time of Samson.

Unfortunately, too many speakers confuse the sitting capacity of their audience with the seating capacity of the dining-room.

I wish more speakers would realize that a good speech consists of a beginning and a conclusion, placed not too far apart.

If they did, fewer people would liken a speech to the horns of a steer – a point here and a point there with a great deal of bull in between.

The points I had to make? Well, welcome everybody. Be happy, all of you. Enjoy yourselves one and all.

Speech No. 2

When I welcomed you at the beginning of the week I immediately tried to put you out of your misery by telling you that I was not a lengthy speaker.

Even so, I must tell you what Lord Mancroft had to say about this.

'A speech,' he said, 'is like a love affair. Any fool can start it, but to end it requires considerable skill.'

I will keep that in mind for the next few moments, and hope that you will afterwards say that his words fell on good ground.

This evening, however, I do want to say how much I personally have enjoyed having you here.

During the week we have met on several occasions, occasions which I myself have thoroughly enjoyed.

I would like to say thank you to all of you for your courtesy and pleasant greetings whenever we met.

I want to say thank you too, to members of our Sailing

Club for their kindness and hospitality. I hope that praise from me, a non-sailor, for all the splendid work they have evidently put in, in connection with this week's activities, will not seem out of place.

At the beginning of the week I told you that we were proud of our sailing facilities. I repeat this tonight but with far greater conviction, for I have since been taken out on a catamaran to watch you racing. Some of the mysteries of your exciting sport were then explained to me, and indeed I sampled a thrill or two.

We know that people who have once been here want to come again. I sincerely hope that this is your experience and that you will visit us regularly.

We have nothing to hide here. I remember hearing a story about a very respectable citizen who had one secret which he wished to keep from everyone. It was that his father had been hanged for murder. He was very successful in concealing this information from all his friends and acquaintances and was a model citizen in every respect.

One day, however, like all other thoughtful people he decided to take out an insurance policy and was given a long application form to fill. One question, however, rather took him aback. It was: 'Are your parents alive. If not state cause of death.'

He got out of this quandary by putting down: 'My mother died of pneumonia at 89 and my father was taking part in an official function when the platform unfortunately gave way.'

We have no secrets here and we have plenty of sources of enjoyment for people who like the sea and country.

Come and explore our County and you will find that time will fly. Time, after all, is relative and months can seem like hours and days can fly like minutes.

I remember hearing about a man who was given six months to live by his doctor. He was very distressed by this and asked: 'Is there anything I can do, doctor?'

The doctor replied: 'Do you smoke?'

'Yes,' said the man.

'Cut it out,' said the doctor. 'Do you drink?'

'Yes,' said the man.

'Cut it out,' said the doctor. 'Do you go out with young ladies?'

'Yes,' said the man.

'Cut it out,' said the doctor.

'Well,' said the man glumly, 'if I do all these things will I live longer than six months?'

'No,' said the doctor, 'But it will seem much longer.'

I hope that you have enjoyed yourselves so much that your time here has flown and that you now feel that you must come again.

Speech No. 3

'Me, learn how to paint? Me, learn to take snaps like in the magazines? Never! It's not in me! I never heard such nonsense!!!' That is an attitude we are all familiar with, isn't it? It is why it gives me so much pleasure to welcome the County Art & Photographic Exhibition to Holyhead once again.

This exhibition will, far more than anything else, help to dispel preconceived prejudices about artistic talent.

Last year the response from the citizens of Holyhead was very good. I hope that this year it will be even better.

Please tell your friends to come along. I am sure everybody will find something here to interest them. The more who come, the more important in the life of our town will this exhibition be.

The general public in this generation are showing far greater interest and appreciation in matters which concern the arts than ever before. Indeed, not so long ago, the only art exhibitions Holyhead ever got were those provided by the old pavement artists. And what specimens they were! No one could be blamed for mistaking these derelict human beings for tramps.

I remember one who was particularly unprepossessing. He had drawn a picture of a five pound note and put his upturned cap, in which there were a few coppers, next to it. Beneath he had written: 'Drawn entirely from memory.'

Today we are accustomed to hearing the word culture on the lips of all sorts of people and in all kinds of places. To be a cultured person is important – no matter what your walk in life; for culture, you know, is the sum of all the many forms of art, of all constructive thought, and of love.

These, in the course of centuries, have enabled mankind to be less enslaved. They raise him above the level of the animal far more than anything else.

I hope that many who visit this exhibition will be prompted to have a go at something similar to the exhibits which are here themselves. I can assure anyone who does, that he is on the threshold of discovering a new facet of himself, and an invaluable sanctuary from the cares and troubles of this mundane, humdrum life.

Actually, the goal does not matter so much as the road and all that one experiences on the way.

In the hope that some of the citizens of Holyhead may, as a result of this exhibition, discover this fact for themselves I am very glad to welcome it to our town.

13
Proposing a Toast

At the conclusion of each of the three speeches which follow I propose a toast.

The first is to the Coxswain, Crew and Helpers of the Holyhead Branch of the National Lifeboat Association. This being such an important body in the life of the port of Holyhead it was considered proper that their toast should be proposed by the town's first citizen.

I came to propose the second toast because I was the President of the Boy Scouts Local Association at Holyhead.

The third speech is one which has been specially written for this book and can be used for any occasion without adaptation.

Speech No. 1

If I were asked to name the dinners which I feel it an honour to attend I would put yours this evening very high on the list. I feel it is a great honour to be asked to attend the annual dinner of an institution which plays such a vital part in the life of our town.

Members of the lifeboat crew are men of action who, I know, will have little patience with long speeches.

It has been said that a speech is like a bad tooth, the longer it takes to draw out, the more the thing hurts.

Well, I certainly don't want to hurt you in any way this

evening. I have no intention of making a long drawn out speech. But it would be churlish of me if I were to let this opportunity pass without saying how very proud we are of you and your record.

Most institutions come in for public criticism by the General Public. I am a member of the district Council and the County Council, and I can assure you that people really enjoy criticizing those two institutions.

That is democracy, I suppose. They elect you so that they can pull you to pieces for the next few years.

But I have never heard a single word of criticism of our Lifeboat.

We land-lubbers stand in awe of the power and might of the oceans. Indeed, a rough crossing to Ireland incapacitates the majority of us, and we think of the sea as the cruel sea. In consequence, we have nothing but admiration for people like you who are prepared to pit their skill and strength against stormy and tempestuous seas for the purpose of saving life.

I remember hearing about a young man who entered a monastery hoping to become a monk. The Order which he wished to join had a strict rule of silence. The abbot told him on his first day that he would be on probation for fifteen years. During that time he would be allowed to speak only once every five years and then only for one minute with the abbot himself.

The young man accepted and was registered as a novitiate.

Eventually the first five years passed and he was summoned to the abbot's study.

'How are you going on, my son?' asked the abbot.

'Oh, all right, thank you, Reverend Father,' replied the young man.

'Have you any complaints?' asked the abbot.

'Well, sir, yes, there is one thing ... the porridge is always cold at breakfast. It would be so much nicer if it were hot.'

'Right,' said the abbot, 'I will see to that. Time is now up.'

The young man left and did not speak again to anyone for

five years. Then he had to go again to the abbot's study.

'How are you going on?' asked the abbot.

'Oh, all right, thank you, sir, I think,' answered the novitiate.

'Have you any complaints?' asked the abbot.

'Well, sir, there is just one thing, the bed is very hard and I find it difficult to sleep. Could I please have a little more straw in my palliasse?'

'Right,' said the abbot, 'I will see to that. Time is now up.' And the young man had to leave.

Another five years passed and the young man went to see the abbot for the last time.

'Reverend Father,' he said, 'my fifteen years probation is at an end. Are you going to accept me as a full member of your Order?'

'Dear me, no,' replied the abbot. 'You have done nothing but complain since you came here.'

Well, we don't complain about the lifeboat people even once in five years and I am happy to pay you the highest tribute this evening. You maintain a high and honourable standard and live up to a noble tradition.

I remember hearing about two soldiers who had to walk all the way from Criccieth to Bangor. It was summer and the day was particularly hot.

After they had walked many miles they saw a woman standing in the garden of her cottage.

'How many miles is it to Bangor?' asked one of the soldiers.

'Oh, about ten,' replied the woman.

They continued walking for another hour and then they met a shepherd.

'How many miles is it to Bangor?' asked the soldier again.

'Oh, about ten,' answered the shepherd.

Feeling very hot and very tired they trudged on for another half-hour. Then they met a schoolboy.

'How many miles are we from Bangor, son?' asked the same soldier.

'About ten, I think,' answered the boy.

The soldier turned to his companion and with a cynical smile remarked: 'Well, mate, we're at least holding our own.'

The Holyhead lifeboat always holds its own and always maintains its high tradition.

It gives me the greatest pleasure to propose the toast to the Coxswain, Crew and Helpers of the Holyhead Branch of the National Lifeboat Association.

Speech No. 2

The Boy Scout movement commands a very warm place in my heart. Always when I think of it, I do so with pleasure and gratitude. Pleasure because, again and again, I savour cherished scouting memories. Gratitude because the movement gave me some of the happiest hours of my life. It brought me into contact with some excellent people of all ages whom I would otherwise never have met.

I am not going to show my gratitude by inflicting a very long speech on you. If I did some of you would afterwards be reminding me of that ancient proverb: 'Gratitude is the least of the virtues and ingratitude the worst of vices.'

It is an odd thing but we human beings are much more interested in the vices of our fellows than in their virtues. Perhaps because of this we tend sometimes to get wrong notions about one another.

One of the oldest maxims among newspaper people is that evil is news, goodness commonplace. They naturally enough exploit this. That is why so many newspapers are full of evil and prophecies of evil things to come.

Now listen to this evil thing:

'Corruption, vice and laxity are the rule today. And this is particularly true of our youth. Our society cannot carry on for the young men of our nation are given up to vain useless pleasures.

They think not at all about tomorrow. They live in foolishness – just for today.

'Woe, woe to our country, the land of our fathers.'

What do you think of that? Typical of the newspapers isn't it? Isn't it what we are hearing and reading everywhere today? This is the gloomy and despondent view too many people have today regarding the future.

But, take heart, those words were not taken from any newspaper. On the contrary they were spoken two thousand five hundred years before the birth of Jesus Christ by King Urukagina of Sumeria.

Don't let such unkind remarks, such prophecies ever depress you. The wiseacres have been saying something like King Urukagina throughout the centuries which have passed since he was alive.

They were saying something similar when I was a boy. Yes, and such things as: 'Spare the rod and spoil the child ... In real old age children are a great comfort, and they help you to reach it much quicker too.'

If people were only to reflect for a few moments on what they are about to say before uttering such damaging things about youth they would realize that it is not so much the youth of the ages that is to blame for the corruption, vice and laxity but those who have reached the so-called age of discretion and responsibility.

All of you know about people who call themselves Punk Rockers.

If you took a walk along the Kings Road, Chelsea any Saturday afternoon you would see collections of them. It is the Punk Rockers Rendezvous.

They all look weird with grotesque hairdos in many shades and spiky styles. They paint odd symbols in striking colours on their faces and some stick saftey-pins through their noses and ears.

In spite of yourself and fearing their reaction you are forced to stare at them, unable to avert your eyes.

People whisper, 'Why do they do it?'

For Display ...? Another Protest ...? less obvious than Protest Marches ...? And easier to misinterpret! Yes, than the Punk Rockers themselves.

But believe me this expresses a fundamental struggle to be different from those – my kind – who have gone before.

They want to do things differently!

People getting on in years will tell you that it is unwise to cast aside the customs and traditions of centuries. Some of them, they will agree, perhaps need modifying, but casting aside, dear me, no! These people maintain that our customs and traditions are the result of the experience of many generations.

Personally, I find that age improves wine, compound interest and little else.

Solomon, you know, first wrote the Song of Songs – a beautiful thing about love; then he wrote Proverbs, which are always being quoted at you, lastly he wrote Ecclesiastes, which to put it mildly is a cynical book. But that is the way of mankind in this world. When we are young we compose songs and write poetry, then later we take to making sententious remarks and lastly, when we are old, we speak of the vanity of things.

But you in the Boy Scout Movement are not concerned with the vanity of things. You go about doing things which are constructive, useful.

You can change the world. And it would change too, if every Boy Scout, every Scouter, every Girl Guide, and every Guider did their best to obey the law of their movements.

> Trusty, Loyal, Helpful,
>   Brotherly, Courteous, Kind,
> Obedient, Smiling, Thrifty,
>   Pure as the rustling wind.

That short verse contains all the tenets of your law. Obey it and you will make the world a better, happier, more godly place. If you live up to your law you will make a far greater, far most lasting change than any of the cults or liveries which are forever being created – and forgotten! The challenge is with you.

In the hope that you will, each of you, henceforth remember this I give you the most important toast of the evening – Scouting.

Speech No. 3

'Judge not that ye be not judged!' I find those words most appropriate this evening.

My toast is that of 'Our Guests'. If I make a porridge of it, I advise the gentleman who has to reply, that to tell me so would be a breach of etiquette. And for anyone else who may be inclined to criticize I quote Sir Francis Bacon: 'In revenge – haste is criminal!' Who knows how long it will be before you will be standing, uncomfortably, where I am.

I hope that all this has softened your hearts, put you in a mood to sympathize with me and approve of the little I have to say to you tonight.

I am very glad to welcome our guests, although gladness and public speaking don't somehow go together with me.

When we entertain we try to be sociable, we bring out the nicest part of our nature. The more we do this, the pleasanter people will find us. This old world of ours will consequently seem a brighter place to them.

We hope that you are enjoying yourselves with us and making friends. I like Abraham Lincoln's definition of a friend. Try it on whoever is sitting next to you – not while I am speaking, of course! Lincoln said that a friend is someone who has the same enemies as yourself.

Speaking of enemies and seeing quite a few bottles around remind me of an experience a friend of mine, who enjoyed his wine, had recently. The minister of his wife's church who was a hell-fire, temperance man called on him one day to remonstrate with him about his occasional alcoholic indiscretions. 'Drink,' he said to my friend, 'drink is your greatest enemy.'

My friend smiled indulgently at him and retorted: 'But padre, doesn't holy writ instruct us to love our enemies?'

Being a minister of religion and preaching seem to be a good number. I heard the other day about three small boys who were bragging about their fathers.

'My father,' said the first, 'writes a few short lines on a piece of paper and calls it a poem, then he sends it away and gets five pounds for it.'

'Huh!' snorted the second little boy, 'my father puts dots on a piece of paper and calls it a song then he sends it away and gets fifty pounds for it.'

'Bah!' exclaimed the third little boy, 'that's nothing! My father writes a sermon on a piece of paper, goes into the pulpit to read it and it takes six men to carry in the money.'

There is a great deal to be said for a good sermon. It helps people in several ways. Some rise from it strengthened. Others awake from it refreshed.

You can say this of speeches too.

I don't expect my speech tonight to have strengthened anybody. On the other hand nobody has gone to sleep either. That really is not at all bad, you know. Give me a moment or two and I'll prove to you that I am a 'finished' speaker – and I'll sit down.

But before I do so I must thank our guests for accepting our invitation. Thank you for being our guests; we are very glad you came.

You other ladies and gentlemen, who are here – thank you for giving me your attention. I ask but one thing more of you, that you rise and drink the toast of 'Our Guests' coupled with the name of Mr.—.

14
Replying to a Toast

In the two speeches which follow I reply to the toast of 'Our Guests'. The occasions were a British Legion dinner and a Sailing Club dinner.

With very little effort anyone can change a speech which has been prepared as a reply to the toast 'Our Guests' to one of proposing that toast, and vice versa.

Speech No. 1

'Do you know what is harder to bear than the reverses of fortune?' is a question once asked by that great soldier Napoleon Bonaparte. He answered it himself with these words: 'It is the baseness, the hideous ingratitude of man.'

Well, I am going to make quite sure that your guests this evening are not accused of ingratitude by starting my speech with saying thank you very much for inviting us here tonight. We are thoroughly enjoying ourselves.

To the gentleman who so ably proposed this toast may I say a special thank you. My fellow guests and I are most grateful to you, sir, for your kind words.

When I decided to come here this evening I sought information about the British Legion. I discovered that it was founded by Earl Haig in 1921 to serve the interests of ex-servicemen.

First of all, you, its members, served your country, and

now you band yourselves together to serve one another.

Your kind has been honoured throughout the centuries.

This evening I pay you my tribute, recalling as I do so the words of Robert Louis Stevenson: 'So long as we love, we serve. So long as we are loved by others we are indispensable; and no man's useless while he has a friend.'

You serve one another. You are true friends. And the only way to have a true friend is to be a true friend.

Now most of you will, I am sure, agree that in the Services one of the most helpful and friendly people is the padre.

One of these was, during the first world war, trying to console a young soldier in the trenches who was trembling with fright.

'Look,' he said, 'stop worrying. If a bullet has got your name on it, you'll get it, come what may. And if it hasn't got your name on it, you won't get it, and you've wasted all this energy worrying over nothing.'

The young soldier thought about this for some moments then he turned to the padre. 'You're right, padre,' he said, 'if a bullet has got my name on it I'm bound to get it whether I worry or not, and I'll take your word for it that those who have some other name on them are not intended for me. But what worries me is those that come over with nothing on them but: 'To whom it may concern!'

In war, as in all 'far' distant events we do not really know what exactly happened, and have to depend on correspondents for information.

In the Falklands, our Armed Forces wrote another page of glory for the annals of our beloved country, manifesting bravery unsurpassed and exhibiting loyalty with patriotism of the highest order.

Many are the stories we have heard and read of our most worthy Task Force. Its members lived up to the highest traditions of our great fighting services. They deserve all honour and glory.

However one of the stories which comes to my mind is about a war correspondent.

This particular war correspondent was a cook on board an aircraft carrier and was at the time well away from the fighting zone.

He had just finished frying masses of eggs for his shipmates. Tired and weary he took up his pen and sat down to write a letter to his sweetheart.

'Dearest Girl,' he wrote, 'for the past three hours shells have been bursting all round me.'

Which, of course, was true!

After war we need benevolence, charity on all sides. Instead we get political expedients. Too often the negotiators are politicians, not statesmen. They think about the next election, not the next generation.

That little boy who was sent to church by his father with 10p and 50p in his pocket will make a good politician when he grows up.

'You are to put whichever you please on the collecting plate,' said his father 'Listen to the sermon and decide whether to give the 10p or 50p in accordance with the impression which that makes on you.'

When the little boy returned from church his father asked him which he had put on the plate – the 50p or the 10p.

'Oh, the 10p,' smiled the boy. 'I was going to give the 50p then I remembered what the preacher had said in his sermon . . .'

'What was that?' interrupted his father.

'The Lord loveth a *cheerful* giver!'

But benevolence is not always appreciated. I am sure that from time to time you have all found this out. Indeed it was only the other day that I was told about an ageing lady who had all through her life practised benevolence. She had been a munificent supporter of many worthy causes. But this did not always please her family.

One day her smart-Alec nephew jibed 'Oh, Auntie you must be on the Sucker's List of practically every charity that was ever thought of.'

'My dear,' she replied, 'I don't mind that at all, provided

you spell it s-u-c-c-o-u-r.'

Succour too, is, I suppose, something you all now need –
succour from me and my speech. Thank you for listening to
me. I wish all of you and your splendid Legion every success.

Speech No. 2

Rule, Britannia, Britannia rule the waves;
  Britons never will be slaves.

So sang the poet in the middle of the eighteenth century.
And it was people like you, who had spent their spare time
messing about with boats, who saved Britons from being
slaves in 1940. The enormous contribution of the weekend
sailors to the evacuation of our troops stranded at
Dunkerque commands an illustrious page in the history of
our island.

Sailing is probably the sport with the greatest useful
potential of all the sports in which we indulge. It touches on
practically everything which the land-lubber does, and a
great deal more besides. You never know when what you
pick up as part-time sailors will be of service to you.

I feel highly honoured at being allowed to join you once
more. It is always a pleasure to mix with a group of people as
congenial and pleasant as our Sailing Club members.

Speaking of conviviality, I remember hearing of two
brothers who were very close to one another. Each evening
they would go to the local public house together and there
each would have a double whisky – an excellent fraternal
procedure of which I thoroughly approve.

Everyone in the 'local' knew of this daily habit and indeed
looked forward to the arrival of the brothers each evening.

One day however one of the brothers told them that they
would not be seeing him any more for a very long time. He
was having to go overseas to work.

The parting was very sad but the brother who was staying
in this country promised he would keep up the old custom

and go to the 'local' at the same time each evening. There would, however, be one difference. In future, he would drink two double-whiskies instead of one – the second one to be his brother's.

This arrangement went on religiously for many months and the inhabitants became accustomed to seeing the lone brother coming in, ordering two double-whiskies, and drinking them.

Then there came a change. The brother came in looking very miserable. Gloomily, he ordered one double-whisky and drank it without pleasure. This went on for two or three evenings until at the end of the week the other customers could stand it no more. 'We've noticed,' they said to the lone drinker, 'that you've changed your ways. Nothing has happened to your brother, has there?'

'No, nothing has happened to my brother,' said the man. 'But something has happened to me – I've gone teetotal.'

Many of you here will know that unfortunately it would be impossible for my brother Thomas and myself to make such a sensible arrangement as the two brothers in that story. He is a Minister of Religion and extremely abstinent. I do my best to redress the balance.

I have told you many times that I do not believe in making lengthy speeches. I am too at a disadvantage here in that I am not really versed in the subject of sailing. It would be useless for me to try to fool experts like you by pretending that I am. Instead, I will tell you about a sailor who went into a public house while he was home on leave. There he met a man with whom he got friendly. Over the drinks they talked, then seemingly in no time, the landlord was calling 'Time, gentlemen, please!'

'Pity,' said the sailor's friend. 'But, never mind. What about coming home with me instead?'

The sailor frowned. 'What for?' he asked.

'Oh, some wine, women and song,' smiled his friend.

The sailor smiled back. 'O.K.,' he said. 'Suits me. All I've had over the past six months is rum, pin-ups and 'baccy.'

There are, evidently, still privations at sea.

Privations and dangers. Ships still get wrecked, and sailors are still washed ashore on desert islands. One of these who had been on one for two years was delighted one morning to see a ship anchor close to and lower a boat which was rowed towards him. As it grounded on the beach an officer threw him a bundle of newspapers.

'We saw your signal,' he said, 'but the Captain thinks you ought to read these, and then let us know if you still want to be rescued.'

Well, one thing seems certain. By this, you will all want to be rescued from me and my speech.

Thank you very much for inviting us as your guests. And thank you particularly Mr. Vice-Commodore for the kind things you said about your guests when you proposed the toast to us. I know I am expressing the feelings of each one of us when I say that sailing club people are good company and that it is always a joy to be with them.

We wish you good sailing and fair weather in all your activities.

15
Fraternity Speeches

Fraternities usually have a dinner after they have gone through their various ceremonies. At this, people make speeches. The candidate is always welcomed and so are visiting brethren. Specimens of speeches which do this follow, together with one which a candidate could use for his reply.

But before we go to them perhaps a brief account of the two most popular fraternities which follow this routine might be found useful.

I refer to the Rotarians and the Freemasons.

Rotarians started their life in Chicago. They were started by businessmen in 1905 to further business service, foster social relations and encourage high ethical standards in business.

Of the four men who started 'Rotary International' one was a coal dealer, one a merchant tailor, one a mining operator and another a lawyer.

Freemasonry is a secret society, having lodges for mutual assistance and social enjoyment all over the world. Roman Catholics have their own fraternity which is called the Knights of St. Columba.

The Freemason's Grand Lodge of England was established in 1707; that of Ireland in 1730 and that of Scotland in 1736.

Speech No. 1 (Welcoming a newly-elected brother)

I heard the other day about a man who was sent to work in a

strange city. At once he started attending one of its churches. He expected that soon the clergyman or some member of the congregation would come to ask him about himself and try to make him welcome there. But no one ever did.

This disappointed him terribly and indeed he would have left and gone to some other church but for the fact that he liked this one and its services very much. Then he had a brainwave. He tore a pound-note in half. On one half he wrote: 'If the clergyman or any member of this church calls on me I will give him the other half of this note. I have been a regular worshipper at your church for weeks now and would be thankful for a little Christian fellowship from anyone there.' He added his name and address and the following Sunday put it on the collecting plate.

Of course, the next day the clergyman arrived full of apologies.

Now you who have become one of us this evening you will never have an experience like that here.

Here a welcome awaits you always. We believe that friendship can only be bought with friendship. There is an old proverb which runs: 'Go often to the house of thy friend for weeds choke up the unused path.' Do please try to attend our meetings regularly. The more we see of you the better we like it and the better we will come to know one another.

We call our members Brothers, a word which you cannot say without at the same time using the word Others. Others are important to us in this fraternity, particularly others less fortunate than ourselves. Never, I hope, do we think of brothers in the way of that small boy who went into a shop where they were giving away toy balloons as an advertising gimmick.

'May I have two, please?' he asked.

'Sorry,' said the manager, 'we can only give one to everyone.'

The little boy's face fell to such an extent that the manager added: 'But perhaps you have a brother at home?'

Although he wanted that other balloon so very badly the

little boy wouldn't lie. Instead he said: 'No, sir, but my sister has a brother.'

Well, we have acquired another brother in you tonight. We welcome you sincerely. If new brethren did not come along our organization would become effete and presently die. It is new blood in the form of newly-elected brethren that keeps us alive and fresh and gives us hope for the future.

That you will be very happy in our midst is the wish of everyone who you will now see rising and drinking to the toast of our newly-elected brother.

Brethren, I give you the toast of our newly-elected brother.

Speech No. 2 (The newly-elected brother replies)

Standing here in front of all of you I remember hearing about a small boy who was looking at a picture of Daniel standing outside the lions' den. 'Daddy,' said the small boy, 'Why is Daniel smiling? Any moment now he'll be thrown into the lion's den, and so far as he knows that will be the end of him.'

'Well,' said his father, 'it's probably because he realizes that when the feasting is over he won't be called upon to say anything.'

Thank you for accepting me as a member of your organization. As yet I do not know a great deal about it. But what little I have assimilated this evening makes me feel that I am going to enjoy being one of you very much.

I will always strive to live up to the principles of your organization so that the two kind gentlemen who proposed and seconded me will never feel that in doing so they made a mistake.

To all of you who have welcomed me I say thank you very much. To you, sir, for the way you proposed this toast, my gratitude.

Speech No.3 (Visiting Brethren)

'Those friends thou hast and their adoption tried,

Grapple them to thy soul with hoops of steel.'

So spoke the Immortal Bard. And so say we. We are always glad to have friends to visit us. One of the advantages of being a member of a fraternity such as ours is that we have many friends whom we have never seen before. For are not friends those who obey the same code and have the same loyalties, ambitions and interests as ourselves?

No one can become a member of our fraternity without first submitting himself to a strict examination and afterwards going through a ceremony of initiation. From this time onwards a new brother obeys the same code and stands for the same loyalties, ambitions and interests as ourselves – indeed he is one of us, and the words of William Shakespeare which I quoted earlier on apply to him.

By visiting one another we get to know our brethren and their ways.

The danger in a fraternity such as ours is that it might become parochial. But visiting brethren bring us news of what takes place at other branches of our fraternity. They bring us new ideas. Discussions with them remind us that our interests should extend beyond the confines of our own town. They prevent us from becoming self-centred. And self-centredness can be a very dangerous thing.

I heard the other day of a very self-centred little girl. One day she ran into the kitchen and threw herself into her mother's arms.

'Mummy,' she wept, 'Michael has broken my dolly.'

'Oh, what a pity,' consoled her mother. 'How did he manage that?'

'He wouldn't give me one of his sweets,' howled the little girl, 'so I hit him over the head with it.'

I suppose that if I do not sit down fairly soon someone will take it into his head to hit me on the head with something.

I am very glad to welcome you, our visitors. Do come again. We are delighted to see you. It is with great pleasure that I propose the toast of 'Our Visitors'.

16
Speeches to Women's Organizations

The speeches which follow are addressed to a Women's Institute and a branch of the Union of Townswomen's Guilds.

They will be well received not only because members of these organizations will approve of the fact that you have troubled to find out something about them, but too, because many members will learn more about their organization from listening to them than they ever did before.

Speech No. 1 (Women's Institute)

The other day a friend of mine produced a very smart hand-sewn leather wallet. 'Look at that,' he said. 'The wife made it. Learnt how at the Women's Institute.'

I had always thought that the Women's Institute was a place where ladies got together once in a while for a cup of tea and a chat, and that's all. After my friend's revelation I started making enquiries and what a surprise I've had.

Your organization is a tremendous force for good in the community. I have discovered that you exist to bring country-women together to learn things which will be of help in their homes. Also you endeavour to improve the conditions of village life.

Every right-thinking person will agree that such objectives are to be commended and should be fostered in every possible way.

You go about it in a most practical fashion at each of your monthly meetings by dividing them into four parts.

Firstly you deal with the business of your association, all of which is carried on, in proper form, by your own members. Then you have a lecture or a demonstration or sometimes a short talk by one of your own members. This is how my friend got his wallet, a major achievement on his wife's part, he thought. And I must say that the two of them had every right to be proud of it. Afterwards you have tea. For getting to know one another and making friends nothing works like a bite to eat and a drink of some sort. Lastly, you have a social half-hour, which you devote to singing, drama, games or some other recreation.

What better methods could anyone conceive to develop in a group a spirit of friendliness, co-operation and initiative?

The three are of the highest importance in any community. You are, I am told, dedicated to developing them amongst yourselves. Let us take them one by one:

Friendship! I quote that brilliant 17th century essayist, Joseph Addison: 'Friendship improves happiness and abates misery by doubling our joy and dividing our grief.' How right he was. There's no doubt that friendships improve every community no matter what its size.

I am glad to say that your faces seem to me to be those of happy people. I am sure that you will readily admit that you owe part of that happiness to your Women's Institute.

Secondly, you aim to develop co-operation among your members. This little story will show you how important co-operation can be.

A few days ago I was talking to a fisherman who told me that he was at long last really prospering.

'I'm very glad,' I said. 'What's happened to improve things?'

'Well,' he said, 'it's like this, I've taken a partner. He's an expert boat handler so he handles the boat and leaves me alone to do the fishing. That way we catch far more than either of us did alone.'

'Freckles,' said someone, 'would be a nice tan if they got together!'

Lastly, you aim to develop initiative.

You do not need me to tell you the importance of initiative. It is a word you are constantly hearing, a quality that is praised everywhere today. The more initiative there is in our country, the more sure it is of prospering. I heard a man put it very neatly the other day: 'Develop initiative,' he said, 'ruts often deepen into graves.'

Not only will you as members of this great organization of yours be better women for developing friendliness, co-operation and initiative, but you will foster them in home to the benefit of your hearths.

Friendliness, co-operation and initiative in the home soon spread out into the streets. Presently your village finds it is a place of developing friendliness, co-operation and initiative.

And what is Britain but a collection of villages. Your potential power is immense.

I wish you all the good luck possible. Do please enthusiastically carry on the good work.

Speech No. 2 (Townswomen's Guilds)

Walter Lippman, an American teacher and editor of stature, said:

'The principles of good society call for a concern with an order of being (which cannot be proved existentially to the sense organs), where it matters supremely that the human person is inviolable, that reason shall regulate the will, that truth shall prevail over error.'

Those words seem to me to encapsulate the aims, and, I would add, ambitions of the Union of Townswomen's Guilds.

I do thank you very much for inviting me to your meeting here today.

I have been telling friends that I was coming, and, do you know, very few of them know much about you? Probably the best I got was: 'They're the townswomen's answer to the countrywomen's Women's Institutes; but don't sing Blake's Jerusalem.' Someone else thought that the Union of Townswomen's Guilds was a society of professional women. None of the men I asked had any idea! Yes, this in spite of the fact that as the Union of Townswomen's Guilds you have been established since 1932. Actually, under other names such as The National Union of Societies for Equal Citizenship, and The National Union of Women's Suffrage Societies you have been going since the end of the last century. Such a record deserves congratulations, and I hasten to pass mine on to you.

You believe, passionately, in education for women.

Emerson, you will remember, said that 'the things taught in colleges and schools are not an education, but the means of education.'

You are for ever trying to discover new methods of attracting the interest of women in scholarship. You endeavour to intrigue them so that they want to get to know more, with the result that they are led to more continuous study.

Education is found to enhance women's contribution to the common good, thus making them better, more valuable citizens.

Moreover, education makes one fitter company for oneself as well as others.

Was it not Aristotle who said: 'Education is an ornament in prosperity and a refuge in adversity'? So you win all ways.

You hold lectures and endeavour to foster interest in music, drama, handicrafts and civics.

'Music', mused Carlyle 'is well said to be the speech of angels' and who can better that?

Drama? Ah, well, I know a little story about drama. There

was this man who said to his friend who enjoyed the theatre: 'Albert, what's the difference between a drama and a melodrama?' Albert took a few moments to compose his thoughts, but presently said: 'Well, in a drama the heroine merely throws the villain over. In a melodrama, she throws him over a cliff!'

Handicrafts? I imagine that handicrafts could kindle in you ladies an interest in the do-it-yourself movement. Some say that this do-it-yourself movement is bad for business. Well, everybody is painting his own house and repairing his own furniture. And there are all kinds of facilities to help the do-it-yourself fan to produce a professional job – like sprays instead of brushes, lambswool rollers, and even drip-dry paint!

A neighbour assured me that a chap in our road is making a fortune out of this do-it-yourself business. He goes around repairing do-it-yourself botches! So, dear ladies, beware!

Your studies of civics show you that every one of us has responsibilities in the community. Prominent among these is our duty to see that homes are built; that families are properly reared; that our sick, needy and suffering are cared for, and that adults, as well as children, are educated.

Further, that as good citizens, we have the responsibility of seeing that action is taken to eliminate disease, accidents, and disasters.

All of these gives us pride in our community, and ourselves. They are desirable everywhere.

Meeting here each month, you get to know one another, and make friends. Friendship is the wine of life. It is Heaven that gives us friends to bless the present scene, which I hope will continue to move forward for you in many ways and ever be a joy to you all. Long may you prosper.

God bless you and your very worthwhile endeavours.

17
Youth

The two speeches which follow are addresses to Youth Clubs. They are not simply social speeches. Each contains a message and is an appeal, for each tries to get the audience to do something which will be to their benefit.

These speeches are included for two reasons. Firstly, because there are today so many youth organizations that one never knows when he might be called upon to address one. Secondly, because they demonstrate how to address the same group on two separate occasions on two aspects of what is basically the same subject – their welfare, or if you prefer it, their good.

A Vicar was recently recalling how as a young curate he had been dismayed at the prospect of preparing two sermons for every Sunday throughout his ministry. That, he calculated, meant about five thousand sermons – he would never have enough to say!

Despondently he went to his ageing vicar to ask how he had managed. 'Oh,' said the old man. It's not so hard, you'll find.'

'But what shall I preach about?' asked my friend.

'God,' said the vicar. 'Just God.'

The popular conception is that addresses about God should be reserved for religious meetings and are inappropriate elsewhere. But add another 'o' and 'ness' to God and you have Goodness. You now have a subject of infinite capacity upon which you can make an endless number of speeches.

Speech No. 1

I have read in one of our national daily newspapers that a number of the young people who go on protest marches do so for very different reasons from those of the organizers. Often, on these marches, people have to sleep a night. Sleeping arrangements, this newspaper maintained, are never those of which Mrs. Grundy would approve. Consequently, in the words of the old silent film captions: 'Sex rears its ugly head.'

This newspaper went on to say that the only campaign in which a number of our young marchers was interested was a sex campaign.

And that is how it always is, isn't it? The majority of the oldies seem to think that their function in life is finding fault with the young. Not only finding fault but misinterpreting practically everything they do.

Why do they do this? Why can't they understand and encourage instead?

Is it because they are jealous of you? Jealous of your youth? Jealous that you have that which they have lost? Could be!

The worst of it is, of course, that you are in the minority. Moreover, that all too soon you may become like them.

Impossible though it may seem to you, they, not so long ago, were like you, full of life, full of enthusiasm, resilient and light-hearted. Your problem is how to avoid generating into vegetables like them.

In the case of the majority of men – and this has been so for generations – you could inscribe on their tombstones:

'This man died at 30.

He was buried at 70.'

You should do your utmost to prevent this tragedy happening to you.

It's easy to say this. Talk is cheap. The problem is how can you avoid degenerating into vegetables. Well, I think, that you must above all else convince yourselves that you are worthwhile. And you are worthwhile providing you are working at something. This country of ours is a good country. It is a good country in which to live, both in sickness and in health. I am not saying that it is the ideal country in which to live. There are probably many ways in which it can be improved still further. That is not the point at the moment. What matters now is that whatever your work is, it matters. It makes you part of the mechanism which keeps this country going.

When you work, use your imagination when thinking about your job, and when you are talking about it to others. I will tell you a story which illustrates this very well.

When a Cathedral was being built a visitor approached three stone-masons and asked each of them what he was doing. The first man said: 'I'm cutting stones.' The second: 'Earning forty pounds a day.' The third proudly said: 'I'm building a wonderful, new cathedral.'

Try to see your work as an integral part of your community. You will find that that helps your self-confidence immensely.

This community of ours is one which improves generation after generation. So keep your ideals alive. Never be afraid to discuss them. You never know what seeds you sow in so doing.

Your ideals and ideas are living things which can grow and multiply only when you discuss them with others.

Therefore take every opportunity to examine them and argue about them publicly.

Remember that you will always be as young as your faith, your self-confidence and hope. It is doubt, fear and despair which make you old, which turn you into a vegetable.

You may not be given the opportunity to make great changes in anything in the world. Indeed such power falls to very, very few. And it is just as true to say that very, very few of us really want it.

Shakespeare gave young people some very good advice you know.

Now, don't let the way school served Shakespeare's work

up to you ruin him for you for ever. Turn to him once in a while. In the peculiar language which he used you will find practically every emotion you will ever experience. Just listen to the verses I am about to read. It may be your first experience of rejecting a prejudice you have formed; that is always a good thing. What I am about to read might cause you to have second thoughts and admit that there is perhaps something in the old boy after all. If you achieve that this evening then its importance in your life is immeasurable.

With Shakespeare's advice to young people I end.

'Look thou character. Give thy thoughts no tongue,
Nor any unproportion'd thought his act.
Be thou familiar, but by no means vulgar.
Those friends thou hast, and their adoption tried,
Grapple them to thy soul with hoops of steel,
But do not dull thy palm with entertainment
Of each new-hatch'd unfledged comrade. Beware
Of entrance to a quarrel; but being in,
Bear't, that the opposed may beware of thee.
Give every man thy ear, but few thy voice;
Take each man's censure, but reserve thy judgement.
Costly thy habit as thy purse can buy,
But not expressed in fancy; rich, not gaudy;
For the apparel oft proclaims the man;
Neither a borrower nor a lender be,
For loan oft loses both itself and friend,
And borrowing dulls the edge of husbandry.
This above all: to thine own self be true,
And it must follow, as the night the day,
Thou canst not then be false to any man.

Speech No. 2 (Relationship with Parents)

Do your parents love you? Whether you believe they do or not, I have no intention of trying to persuade you, one way or the other. Instead, I will tell you just when you will find this out for yourselves. It won't be for some time yet.

Actually, not until the grave closes over them or you become parents yourselves. Then you will know!

I am not being cynical when I tell you not to worry unduly about this. There is nothing new in it. It is not peculiar to your generation. On the contrary this has been so as far back as history takes us.

Shakespeare had something to say about it. He wrote:

'Crabbed age and youth cannot live together
Youth is full of pleasance, age is full of care;
Youth like Summer morn, age like winter weather;
Youth like Summer brave, age like winter bare.'

Actually the relationship between youth and age has improved since Shakespeare's day. We all live together more amicably now.

Mark Twain, the great American author, used to say that when he was fourteen his father was so ignorant he could hardly stand to have him around. But when he got to be twenty-one he was astonished at how much his father had learned in those seven years.

Today, your parents may seem to you to be people who keep on saying: 'Now when I was young,' yet never show any sign of having ever been young themselves.

But, believe me, that is how their parents seemed to be to them when they were young.

Today, parents are, in my opinion, more tolerant of the behaviour of their sons and daughters than ever before. I wonder, however, whether you are as tolerant of your parents as they had to be of theirs!

I heard recently of a father who was found sitting on the front steps of his home at three in the morning by a policeman.

'What are you doing here?' demanded the policeman.

'Oh,' said the man, 'I've lost my key so I'm waiting for my children to come home and let me in.'

But few parents stay out 'partying' until the early hours of the morning. I wonder how you would react if your parents started doing this and you had to wait up until they came in?

Even if you didn't wait up for them! Would you not soon be asking such questions as, 'Where have you been? What have you been doing?'

Are not these questions precisely those which they now ask you?

How would you react to their answers, I wonder?

And how long would it be before you started having doubts?

Would your faith be as strong as theirs?

The other day a woman sent her small son for 2 lb. of apples. Later, she telephoned the greengrocer to complain that she had weighed the apples and found that there was only a pound and a half in the bag.

'I know that my scales are correct,' answered the greengrocer. 'Why don't you now weigh your son?'

What we all need – you the young people of this generation and those of us who are older – is tolerance.

And this even more so when you are part of a one-parent family. When there are two parents they work off a lot of the aggro of living on one another, and you the juniors in the union have two to work on, sometimes even to work against one another, and you do that when too much critical attention is focused on you and your doings. But in a one-parent family you get all the works. . .! Your parent has no one else to blame for life, consequently the candid camera is always on you.

No matter how many the ingredients which make your family, the key-note to its harmony is tolerance. There are, you all know, black and white keys on a piano. Play them together thoughtlessly, without regard to any rules, and you get discord. But if you understand music and spend some time practising you can, with the same black and white keys, produce sweet harmonies which move the soul.

If young people and their parents were to spend time studying one another and trying to understand one another then far more homes would be places of sweet harmony.

Why not try? You start. You'll be surprised at how quickly your people will respond.

18
Old Age

A feature of Holyhead is that it has four Old People's Clubs. As Chairman of the Council I had at Christmas to go around them all. In addition to this, I attended at least three parties given by other organizations to Old Age Pensioners.

I would have enjoyed all this much more had it not been for the fact that I had to make a speech at each of them. The actual delivering of the speeches did not disturb me – they were all appreciative audiences. It was the preparation of the speeches which became a nightmare. You see, I knew that a small hard core of pensioners would attend the lot and these would quickly recognize a speech which I had delivered before. Their comments afterwards would, I felt, be – shall we say uncomplimentary? There was only one thing to do. Prepare a new speech for each occasion. Believe me, when I came to the seventh I was really scraping the bottom of the barrel.

Don't worry, I am not going to inflict them all on you. Indeed there is but one of these Christmas speeches included in what follows. In it there are some useful epigrams about Christmas and Christmas presents. I have put it the first of the three.

Of the other two speeches which follow, one is a straightforward address to old people, and the other is one which I delivered at a party to celebrate the second anniversary of an Old People's Club.

Speech No. 1

Whenever I receive a card from your honorary secretary asking me to attend a Millbank Old People's Club Function those letters 'R.S.V.P.' at the bottom remind me of a certain Mr. Isaacs whose daughter was getting married.

All the arrangements had been made and Mrs. Isaacs was telling her husband about them.

At each expense he got sadder and sadder. By the time she came to the invitation cards he was really miserable.

'What's this nonsense?' he asked pointing to the letters 'R.S.V.P.' at the bottom of one of the cards.

'Ah,' said his wife, 'that's where your Rebecca has been clever. That means, "Reply Soon Vith Presents".'

This is the time for presents, Christmas presents. May you all receive many.

Someone has said that Christmas presents can be divided into two classes – those you don't like, and those you don't get.

Well, I hope you get the sort of presents you like.

Last week I heard a man say that what he liked about Christmas was that you can make people forget the past with a present.

And that's not a bad idea for all of us this Christmas. This is the season when everyone speaks and reads about goodwill. It is the time of times to redress wrongs and repair damaged relationships. Use it.

What did Dickens call it? A kind, forgiving, loving time.

I hope you find it so. I am very grateful to you for asking me to your party, and take this opportunity of wishing you, one and all, a merry Christmas followed by a very happy new year.

Speech No. 2

Life has no pleasure nobler than that of friendship. This is a truth which you Senior Citizens of our town discovered a long time ago. That is why you join one another here so frequently. Seeing you so happy is a pleasant experience and an object lesson to all of us who are honoured to call on you.

People who are getting on in years have found out what is the secret of serenity and happiness. This is something which is denied the young and the middle-aged. Perhaps if we were to come and see you senior citizens oftener we would discover what this secret is. Part of it I am sure is that happiness is something you cannot chase and catch. Young people spend their life chasing it, but somehow they never quite get hold of it.

I think that I am now old enough to realize that happiness is a gift which comes quietly when one least thinks about it. A good example of this is to be found in a pretty little story called 'Golden Windows'. It tells of children playing in the front garden of their home one evening and seeing a palace with windows of gold on a far-off hill. They decide to go to this palace, so they climb their garden wall, walk down their street, through some brambles, across some marshes until finally they reach the hill and climb it.

But at the top disappointment awaits them. They find that their palace with the golden windows is only an old ruin whose windows have been touched by the setting sun.

They are now very sad so they turn to go home; but there, in the distance, behold they see their house. From here though that has golden windows.

Young people strive hard, yet, too often, lose sight of the things that are really worthwhile.

As we grow old we come to realize what things have real value. One of them is companionship. Surely companionship is the great benefit which comes from these clubs.

Companionship transcends even likes and dislikes. I heard a short time ago a silly story about a man who walked into a café and asked the waitress to bring him grape-fruit juice, half water with seeds in it; scrambled eggs, leathery and watery; toast burnt to a frazzle and a pot of luke-warm tea with the leaves floating in it.

The waitress stared at him in amazement for a moment or two then habit reasserted itself and she asked mechanically: 'Anything else, sir?'

'Yes,' he nodded. 'Just sit opposite me and nag me. You see I'm homesick!'

Well the food you get here is much better than that to which that man was accustomed. And no one nags at you here. Here you may indulge in a little harmless leg-pulling to while away the hours and keep one another interested. Interest, by some means or another, is something you must keep alive because it keeps you alive.

May you continue to find your club and companions ever interesting. Whilst you do so this place is a priceless tonic.

Thank you for asking me here. God bless you all.

Speech No. 3

I am here tonight to wish your club a happy birthday.

Now, I myself have reached that stage in life where I like to have my birthdays remembered but not my age.

But then, of course, I am older than two. I suppose I am what is called middle-aged, which is when you start eating what is good for you and not what you like.

I hope your club has many, many more birthdays.

This must be a great day for those who conceived the idea of building these premises. Your baby is two years old today, and a robust, healthy baby it looks to me. Everyone who has had anything whatsoever to do with bringing it to life and rearing it this far must be very proud.

The more I think about these clubs for our senior citizens the more I like them.

This is a place you can come to when you want peace and quiet. It is a place where you can come to tea every Thursday and chat with people of your own age group.

You can talk about old times – the people you knew in the past, perhaps when you were boys and girls.

I find tracing back families to be a most interesting diversion. I am sure that you have great fun when you indulge in it. If this is not already one of your pastimes I strongly recommend it to you. Try it one afternoon. You will be astonished at how quickly that afternoon passes. You will marvel at how characteristics are passed on by fathers and mothers to their children. And because you are older than I you will be able to do this in much the same way as the Children of Israel – unto the third and fourth generation.

Indeed you will realize, not for the first time I'm sure, how true the Bible is, not only of the Children of Israel but of all people living in a community – of humanity as we know it.

As you think on these things you will discover the truth of that old paradox: 'The boy is the father of the man.' That is to say a pleasant, kind, obliging boy grows up to be a pleasant, kind, obliging man. It is true of the girls too, of course. The selfish, self-centred, gossipy little girl grows up to be a selfish, self-centred, gossipy woman, and continues to make things difficult no matter where she goes! Of course, there are no selfish, self-centred, gossipy little boys! They are all perfect. Indeed I was surprised to hear one the other day when asked what a grandmother was, say: 'A grandmother is an old lady who keeps your mother from spanking you.'

Another diversion which you would find interesting is that of tracing how well, or badly, the boys and girls who were clever at school did in after-life.

You can talk too about Holyhead as it was. Some of you will no doubt remember our Harbour of Refuge sheltering from tempest hundreds of sailing vessels.

You can exchange recollections about famous wrecks and rescues; about defunct shipping companies which at one time were very important in the town.

Think back to the days of your youth. Who were the personalities and characters in the town then? Which people amused, interested or annoyed you in those days?

Only last week I was complaining to a friend that there didn't seem to be any characters like those of my youth around today. He cut me short. 'Don't talk nonsense,' he said. 'You and I are the characters today.' Be that as it may, the past is very important. It is tradition. It is something which ought to be preserved.

It would be an excellent thing for the town if you kept a record of your reminiscences, in writing or on tape. Generations to come could then read or hear them. They would get to know better the place which gave them birth. Yours, and the memories of those who went before you, are our heritage. They are what makes Holyhead individually different from any other town, and to some of us, the best town in the world.

May I congratulate you on looking so well, all of you. Being the senior citizens of the town suits you, each one of you. You have a place of honour in our community. Make as much use as you can of your club. Keep on being interested in one another and indeed in as many other things as you can.

May God continue to bless you all.

19
Welcoming Foreigners

The first of the speeches which follow was prepared for delivering to a party of Americans visiting our country.

I have included it because these days one never knows when he may be called upon to address visitors from foreign lands, and it shows the sort of thing one should try to put over on such occasions.

If you are ever asked to address foreign visitors always be as polite and charming as you can, no matter what is your personal opinion of the individuals or their country. Always remember they will judge our country by the impression you make on them.

The Speech

'The United States of America and Great Britain are two nations separated by a single language.' I am sure you have all often heard that quotation. It seems to me to be quite true too. For instance: we don't eat candy, we call that sweets; we don't play checkers, but draughts. Our counterfeiters are coiners; elevators here are lifts, and peanuts we call monkey nuts.

Your men wear undershirts, ours vests. You shine your shoes, we polish ours. Garters here are suspenders, while what you call suspenders we call braces.

Another thing which separates us is, of course, the Atlantic; but with today's magic carpet, which we call Concorde, and those man-made marvels up there circuiting the earth and beaming pictures of events as they occur from one side of the ocean to the other, science has diminished it so that its effect today is only slightly more limiting than the English channel was decades ago.

It now takes less time to travel by air from London to New York than it does to get from London to Edinburgh by train.

I hope that you are enjoying the look you are taking at us. The more your nation and mine visit one another, the better it is not only for our two nations but for all the nations of the world.

I dare say you've noticed we do some things differently from you. For instance, I'm sure you'll say we drive on the wrong side of the road. Er ... we call it the left-hand side!

No doubt too, you've found some things about us which have caused you amusement. The uniforms some of our military men wear; for example: The Beefeaters in Tower of London; the Chelsea Pensioners in Sir Christopher Wren's magnificent Chelsea Barracks; the breast-plated Household Cavalry on Horse Guards Parade and the busbies of the Guardsmen on sentry duty outside Buckingham Palace.

There is, however, one uniform we both identify the moment we land in our respective countries – the Customs Officer's. He is there watching, no matter what time we arrive. And he can spot-check passengers even after they have passed through the Green Channel, as a friend of mine discovered.

He was already clutching the regulation duty-frees in the usual plastic bag; so started to pray.

'Have you anything to declare?' demanded the Customs man eyeing my friend's jumbo-sized suitcase.

'Nothing', said my friend, 'only clothes – used clothes!' But he had to open it, and the Customs man started to rummage. Suddenly he stopped. His hand had touched something hard; and in a moment he brought it out – a bottle of brandy!

'I thought you said it only contained clothes!' he said menacingly.

'Yes, that's right,' said my friend. 'That's my nightcap!'

The differences between us are, thank heaven, actually of little consequence. They are in no way sinister! All they do is provide our two countries with national character. In essentials we are one.

Our conceptions of freedom, justice, government and democracy are similar.

We like to think that you are like us and that we are like you. Two nations separated by one language, I said, earlier on. Yes, but welded together by history, war and mutual experiences. We observe the same moral code, our ideal is peace and goodwill among men. So long as we stand side by side at the van of the English-speaking peoples, the torch of freedom will continue to burn.

I don't think anyone can improve on the way a Red Indian in your Army during the last war described the relation between your country and ours. 'You know,' he said, 'when our countries smoked the Pipe of Peace together they sure did inhale.'

And that is why we are glad to see you. The more we learn about one another as individuals and representatives of vocations, professions, trades or occupations, the better we will understand one another. Understanding, you know, begets tolerance and the more tolerance any one of us can foster in the world the better it will be for us and our children.

There is no Pipe of Peace here for me to smoke, but there is a drink. It is with affection that I drink to you and your great country. To America!

The second is a speech of welcome to the delegation from a French town 'twinned' with ours and is therefore more personal.

Speech No. 2

Bienvenu et soyez le bienvenu, which for others who like

myself are monoglots means: 'Welcome, and it's nice to have you with us.'

Madamoiselle Smith, une femme professeur, pour notre lycée has very kindly consented to translate what I say into French. I will speak slowly so that she can do this, and everyone will understand – I hope!

Her task, I am told will be simplified, because, unlike French, so many English words have a number of different meanings. Take, for instance, the English word, fast. If in French I said I was *vite* – I would be fast; or if I said I was *attaché*, I would still be fast; or if I confessed to being a *dissipateur* – a spendthrift – they would again call me fast; or were I not eating – *ne manger* – that too would be fast – a fast.

The reports which reach me are that many of you are fast learners and already converse in English as though you were Englishmen, in accents which have certainly improved from *atroce*.

Congratulations, we are delighted. I am told too that great progress is also being made by our own people who speak French, no matter to what degree. These are, of course, the more obvious benefits which the Twinning of our towns produces.

But language is not the only thing that has improved from our Twinning. It has encouraged a number of our citizens to visit other parts of *la Belle France* and they have had many surprises. One of these tourists was telling me about the time he went to Paris. He had gone to the magnificent Luxembourg Gardens. There he got a considerably greater thrill than at the Folies Bergère, for on a terrace there stood a row of life-size statues of the Queens of France in weathered stone. And one of these bore the name Mary Stuart. Yes, our own Mary, Queen of Scots. It took him moments to blow away the cobwebs from his memory and remember that she was the widow of the son of your great François the First, who did so much to encourage the arts in your country. For him during that moment, for the first time in his life, history lived.

Many of you, I am told will have to fast when you return to France. Your much-vaunted French cooking has to some extent, this week, lost the Grand Prix. That has instead been generously awarded to our bacon, eggs, toast and marmalade. The British breakfast, along with our roast beef and Yorkshire pudding have won over many discerning stomachs.

And, of course, there is the British pub with its cold refreshing beer. I have heard whispers that some prefer it to today's Bistro. No one, though, has said that he prefers beer to wine. Indeed, I understand that you have no difficulty in converting most of our hosts to changing to it. And was that not always so?

Our people have taken you around to see the sights – some of our light industries, and the vessels which ferry people across the Irish Sea to Eire. Industries, schools and commercial institutions you found were as routine here as at home. Our way of life has many basic similarities.

Some of you were taken to see our nearest stately home, Plas Newydd, which is on the other side of the Isle of Anglesey. When you heard the name of the soldier to whose memory the nearby tall column was erected you insisted on climbing to its top to inspect. To those of you who did not go, the statue at the top is that of the first Marquis of Anglesey. You may have heard of him. As Lord Uxbridge your forbears shot off one of his legs – that was at Waterloo!

Yes, it is true to say that we have not been the great friends and permanent allies that we are today, and for many years fought one another. Be that as it may, no matter. Fighting side by side in two world wars has so cemented our relationship that we have become permanent allies.

Last Sunday, you organised a simple and very touching ceremony at our War Memorial, which pleased the town very much. As your Mayor wearing his sash of office laid your wreath on the Memorial the words of one of our modern writers, Howard Spring, rang in my ears! 'Love', he wrote 'for the same thing never makes allies. It's always hate for the same thing'.

May we ever hate the same evil. It is in your national character to love Freedom, Equality & Brotherliness and to fight to the death for them. And it is in ours too.

Ladies and Gentlemen, I ask you to be up-standing and drink a toast to our honoured guests.

Vive la France.

20
Appeals

The first of the three speeches which follow is an appeal on behalf of an imaginary organisation concerned with child welfare. The other two are appeals on behalf of the Freedom from Hunger Campaign, and the charity, Help The Aged.

The Freedom from Hunger Campaign speech was delivered from of all places a pulpit, to an audience of about a thousand.

The occasion was a concert at which artistes of B.B.C. fame sang solos and duets. Other items were presented by one of the town's best choirs. The whole thing was a great success, financially and culturally. At it I learned a lesson: although I got laughs for my crack that I felt a mistake had been made and that my reverend Brother ought to be in the pulpit, not me, and for the one about my figure, my other jokes fell a little flat. The audience was as though it were too embarrassed to laugh.

When, however, I began to 'preach' on behalf of the Freedom From Hunger Campaign they were delighted and listened as though spellbound. Perhaps they felt they ought not to laugh too often in church, even though it was a non-conformist church and had none of the religious furnishings of more demonstrative persuasions.

You, however, might think that the other jokes did not merit a laugh – perish that thought!

The Help The Aged speech I have made in varying forms, in many places to many differing audiences – schools, churches, organisations, such as women's institutes, Lions,

Rotarians, etc. It has always been well received and highly profitable to the charity.

Speech No. 1

'It is more blessed to give than to receive,' are words which have caused men to ponder and act generously throughout the Christian era.

Benevolence is a virtue of the highest order. It has brought immeasurable benefits to humanity.

One of the attributes of benevolence is sympathy; indeed sympathy is the force which triggers off benevolence.

I am sure that your sympathy will be triggered off when I tell you the story of little Ellen Smith.

Until six months ago her father was abroad with the navy. Ellen, her mother, and three other children lived with her grandmother. Her mother had never wanted her. Her grandmother did though, and protected her so that she was happy enough. But within the past nine months two calamities occurred in Ellen's life. Firstly, her grandmother died, and secondly, her father was discharged from the navy and came home to live. He disliked Ellen, and felt her very being an insult to him. She had red hair and he knew of no one in his family who had red hair. Because of this, and the fact that his wife had no time for her, he got to thinking that Ellen was not his child.

Soon he was beating her with a cruel belt. He would keep her locked up alone for days in an attic bedroom in which there were no amenities, not even a light. He made the poor child's life a hell on earth. And in that hell she would still be, if a kindly neighbour had not reported her plight to the society on behalf of which I am appealing this evening.

Ellen Smith now lives at one of its homes. She has become a happy, healthy child, full of life. Slowly, she is forgetting the nightmare days which followed her grandmother's death and her father's homecoming.

I wish you could see her both now, and as she was before she went to the home. If you could, I am sure she would touch your hearts. But because it would be wrong of us to make a spectacle of little Ellen Smith I cannot let you see her even as she is today.

The society which is looking after her needs funds, funds to carry on its excellent work of which I have given you but one example. I assure you that there are thousands of others.

Will you please give generously? Your support is sorely needed.

Thank you for listening to me so attentively. I hope I have shown you that this society is worthy of your support and will now ask the stewards to go round and collect your contributions ... I assure you that no penny of what you give will be wasted. Thank you very much.

Note

The ending of this appeal depends on how you are collecting the money, of course.

You will notice that the appeal itself is really the story of Ellen Smith, a victim of child-cruelty until she was rescued by the society on behalf of which the appeal is made. This is known as a human-interest story. You will find that it is easily the best way of making such an appeal. People understand a human story much better than the recital of a long list of statistics. What is more they respond far more generously to the appeal in connection with which it is told.

Speech No. 2

Standing here, looking around, I am inclined to wonder whether a mistake has not been made. Have you not got the wrong member of my family here? Surely, this is my reverend brother's forum.

I wonder too, what I am doing appealing for Hunger Relief with a figure like mine!

For some time before coming here I was at a loss to know why there should be a chairman at all at a concert like this.

Eventually somebody told me. 'You are,' he said, 'like the sprig of parsley that's served with the fish course.'

I don't think he intended that I should interpret this as meaning that I am decorative. And I certainly am not saying that our wonderful artistes look like fish!

But you will, I trust, pardon me the irresistible pun: it's a whale of a concert!

And you are a whale of an audience. Thank you for buying tickets. Thank you for coming. Without you all the effort behind this evening would have been in vain. And we would have felt like the mother who said to her little girl: 'I've tried so hard. I've done everything I can to make you good, to make a success of you. But all my efforts have been wasted and I am made to look a fool.'

The little girl turned on her mother and said callously: 'Mother, you are a failure!'

Thanks to you, we this evening have not been a failure.

Our compère, choir, artistes have all been splendid too, haven't they?

We are grateful to the gentlemen in the choir, Mrs. Gaynor Williams, their accompanist, and Mr. Dewi Francis, their conductor. You are always ready to give your splendid services free to any good cause. Listening to you has been a thrilling experience.

The individual artistes and their accompanist deserve our thanks too. Even those who are not musically minded must surely applaud your very fine performance. Thank you, Mrs. Enid Thomas, Mr. Richard Rees and Mr. Richie Thomas for coming here at a reduced fee, and thank you Miss Olwen Lewis for giving your excellent services free.

There are some other good people who I would like to thank too. The Minister, Deacons and Members of this Church for allowing us the use of it.

Is there anybody else? Oh, yes, the compère and the organizers.

Everybody here tonight is twice blessed. Not only have we had a most enjoyable evening, but we have too the satisfaction of knowing that all the money made as a result of this concert will go to one of the most worthy causes on earth today – The Freedom From Hunger Campaign, a charity which has been commended to us by the highest in the land.

Now there are two forms of charity – one alleviates and the other cures. The first is often prompted by sentiment, the second ... Christianity.

The Freedom From Hunger Campaign is, of course, in the second category.

Officials of this organization see to it that aid is given to the needy in two parts. The first part consists in providing them with sufficient food for a healthy life for the time being. And, believe me, these communities are in dire need. They are not simply underfed or undernourished. Many of their members are literally starving. Too often are they a pitiful prey to hideous diseases from the day they are born, throughout their primitive, insanitary lives, until they reach their inevitably early graves.

And all this is so unnecessary in the world with all the knowledge and resources at its command today.

This is where the second part of the work of the organization which we are supporting tonight comes in. Officials of the Freedom From Hunger Campaign advise, train and – with funds supplied by good people like you – equip these communities so that in the years ahead they will eventually be self-supporting. Henceforth, they will be kept on the road to prosperity. No longer will they need charity from ourselves or anybody else.

Without our aid their situation is hopeless. And what a shamefully sad thing that is to say, especially when you hear that Freedom From Hunger Campaign field-workers say that there are really no hopeless situations. No, they are all situations in which people have grown hopeless by being in them.

The Freedom From Hunger Campaign brings hope to

these. Hope that the future holds for them a better, healthier, more fortunate life. No longer will they be worse off than animals. Their rising generation starts to be more important, more significant. Soon they are like the early Children of Israel, full of hope – planning for the third and fourth generation.

Anyone who helps any human being from degradation, evil superstition or circumstances is surely doing God's work. Anyone who improves the lot of humanity in any part of this old world of ours glorifies God. It is worthy, holy work.

In various ways, you – each one of you – by being here tonight have contributed to this high calling. Thank you.

Speech No. 3

Charity begins at home ... but should not end there, is the kind of thinking which prompted Cecil Jackson-Cole to found Help the Aged. Already he was co-founder of Oxfam and was abroad in connection with its work when he had this vision:

In the world there were millions of refugees of all ages. For the young and middle-aged there was hope – possible rehabilitation; they were able to start a new life. But for the aged; what did the future hold for them? They were too old to start again. There was not time. Many would be gone ... within twelve months! So why not do something for them, here and now? What could be done would have to be done at once. An old Latin proverb avers: 'He twice gives who gives quickly.'

And so in 1961 Cecil Jackson-Cole inaugurated the charity which he called 'Help the Aged Refugees Appeals' to bring positive relief to old people caught up in both man-made and natural disasters.

That is how the national charity for whose support I am now appealing to you was started.

Today it is called Help the Aged and it gives aid to sick, needy or destitute aged people the whole world over, regardless of race, caste or creed.

In our country it has been foremost in establishing housing for the aged. It is in the front line of endowing research by medical science into the needs of the elderly, and, in this field, it feels that a great deal more can be done, and needs to be done, to deter the deleterious effects which advancing years so frequently have upon us. This is not an airy-fairy notion, but the considered opinion of medical men who now, as a result of hefty Help the Aged endowments, research the mysteries of gerontology. This means that when you support Help the Aged each of you is supporting a campaign which could be helpful to you yourself. So, tonight, be kind to yourselves, and give generously ... Please.

There are many other ways by which Help the Aged improves life for our aged. It considers Day Centres to be of prime importance, and supports these in more than one way all over our land. The great bogey of old age is loneliness. At these Day Centres it is never allowed across the threshold. So important does it consider Day Centres that Help the Aged often provides a minibus to get aged people to them, even when it itself does not run the Day Centres.

I could go on and on, but the clock is already ahead of me and I have yet to tell you about some of its work overseas. Why don't you yourselves send a post-card to Help the Aged to ask for more details? Just address it to: Help the Aged Headquarters, London, or, better still, get the full address from a telephone directory.

Abroad there is unbelievable poverty, such as we in Britain know nothing. Out there people really are starving. All the problems that we have, they have – but magnified many times.

Take, for instance, housing. In Calcutta they beg for a blanket – that will be their house, their shelter and most prized possession, until they are taken, wrapped up in it, on their final journey to the burning ghat.

In Africa water is the eternal problem. With grants from Help the Aged wells are sunk and water, not only for drinking but irrigation too, brings the aged better lives.

Africa and India have tremendous medical problems. One for which Help the Aged has done a great deal is to do with cataracts. It finances hospitals doing ophthalmic work so that those who were recently blind can now see. For places like Somalia it has even sent out special medical teams to cope with ophthalmic operations.

Welfare work continues in South America. There, Help the Aged initiates and supports self-help schemes, such as a laundry in Colombo, a job-creation scheme in Peru, and so on.

At Christmas time the very poor of the Third World in many places bless it for its Christmas Meals Programme which makes sure that thousands have a special meal and celebration at this time.

When disaster strikes, whether man-made, as in war or insurrection, or as the result of natural causes, such as earthquakes and floods Help the Aged is in the forefront with material help.

I have tried to give you an all-round picture of the work which Help the Aged does. It is, I know, sketchy, but in the short time at my disposal whatever I say must of necessity be inadequate.

Please, though, do as I asked earlier on: Write to Help the Aged Headquarters, London, for more information. The telephone directory or British Telecom will provide you with the full address if you would prefer that.

Presently, there will be a collection. Please, please, I beg of you, give to it all you dare.

Whatever you give will, I assure you, be very gratefully received, and most faithfully applied.

Thank you.

21
Opening an Event

The opening of a Garden Fête, Sale of Work or Bazaar requires little in the way of a speech. Their organizers want the things opened as quickly as possible so that the public can circulate and spend their money.

I suggest that you say something like this:

The Speech

'The customer is always right,' was once the motto of many business undertakings. From the kind and cheerful looks on the faces of this afternoon's stall-holders I feel sure that they will treat all their customers with the utmost courtesy and consideration, even should they decide that they are not always right.

To me they look really anxious to meet you – all of you. I wouldn't be surprised if some of them are now thinking that I should hurry up so that they can get down to business!

But I too have a function in the business side of this afternoon's proceedings. Indeed from me you get the 'Commercial'!

Not only do I recommend everything here and persuade you that you have need of the things on all the stalls, but, I am too, able to assure you that every penny you spend is wanted and will be put to good use.

Your church cannot carry on in the way it does without

functions such as this. So please spend as much as you can here. Be extravagant! Spoil yourselves!

Now there are great numbers of people to thank. There always are in a function such as this. The best way for me to do this is by saying: We thank everyone who has helped or is helping in any way whatsoever to make this Garden Fête possible.

I myself wish it the greatest possible success.

In the hope that it tops all previous efforts I have great pleasure in declaring it open.

22
Politics

This book is not concerned with party politics, and the making of a proper political speech is beyond its scope. That is a job for the 'expert'. On occasions, however, an inexperienced person is asked to propose or (more briefly) second a vote of thanks to some speaker or speakers at a political meeting. What follows may be helpful. It can be adapted to any political occasion. All you have to do is substitute the name of your party for Party 'A' and another for Party 'B'.

Speech No. 1

It gives me great pleasure this evening to propose a vote of thanks to our speakers. Listening to them has, I am sure, been an enlightening experience for all of us.

A short time ago the 'A' Party and ours held public meetings in the same hall within a week of each other.

The son of the caretaker of that hall saw in this an opportunity to sell his four puppies. He put them in a box on which he wrote 'Puppies For Sale' and stood with them at the entrance to the hall. A member of the 'A' Party decided that one of them would be nice for his son. 'Are they "A" puppies?' he asked.

'Oh, yes, sir!' answered the boy.

And so a puppy was sold.

The following week when our party was holding its meeting the boy was there again with the remaining puppies.

A member of our party, attracted by them, asked him: 'Are they "B" puppies, son?'

'Yes, sir,' said the boy.

Unfortunately for him though, the man who had bought a puppy the previous week was standing close by, and heard him.

'Wait a moment,' said this man. 'Last week you told me they were "A" Puppies!'

'That's right, sir,' said the boy. 'But these aren't – these ones have got their eyes open.'

I am sure that there are many here this evening who have had their eyes opened by what our speakers have said. Indeed, having listened carefully, I confess to seeing more clearly myself.

If the case for our party is presented all over the country in as efficient a manner as we have heard tonight, and people listen properly, then there is no doubt as to the outcome of the next election.

Ladies and gentlemen, I formally move a vote of thanks to our speakers. May they have great good luck and much success always.

Speech No. 2

It gives me pleasure to second the vote of thanks proposed by Mr. Smith.

Listening to our most able speakers I couldn't help thinking that it is three bones which will see our campaign through to a successful conclusion: the wishbone, the jawbone and the backbone. The wishbone because it will keep our goal foremost in our mind. The jawbone because it is by talking about our campaign and asking questions about that of others that we will convince others that right is on our side. And the backbone because that will keep us at it until we reach our goal.

The old African witch-doctor can do wonderful things with his bones. We can too if every one of us uses the three which I have mentioned for the good of the party.

I now formally second the vote of thanks and I am sure you would all like to demonstrate your appreciation of the efforts of our speakers in the time-honoured way. (Applaud!)

INDEX TO PARTS II & III

PART IV

Epigrams, Stories and Anecdotes

In the pages which follow there is a collection of epigrams, stories and anecdotes with which you can make new speeches or from which you can take material to refurbish one of the specimen speeches which are to be found in this book.

I have put the epigrams first. I have done this because when I come to prepare speeches I find it more convenient to have the epigrams, from which I often obtain ideas for themes, together and separate from the stories and anecdotes which I use to illuminate what I say.

Epigrams

ACHIEVEMENT, PERSEVERANCE, SUCCESS, DESTINY

1. They conquer who think they can. *John Dryden*.

2. The men whom I have seen succeed best in life have always been cheerful and hopeful men, who went about their business with a smile on their faces and took the changes and chances of this mortal life like men, facing rough and smooth alike as they came. *Charles Kingsley*.

3. The world continues to offer glittering prizes to those who have stout hearts and sharp swords. *Lord Birkenhead*.

4. Everything comes to him that hustles while he waits. *Thomas A. Edison*.

5. Greatness is not achieved by never falling, but by rising every time we fall. *Confucius*.

6. It is often the last key on the ring that opens the door.

7. To be great is to be misunderstood. *R. W. Emerson*.

8. A life of ease is a difficult pursuit. *W. Cowper*.

9. The longer I live the more keenly I feel that whatever was good enough for our fathers is not good enough for us. *Oscar Wilde*.

10. If you have great talents industry will improve them; if you have but moderate abilities, industry will supply their deficiency. *Sir Joshua Reynolds*.

11. The way for a young man to rise is to improve himself every way he can, never suspecting that anybody wishes to hinder him. *Abraham Lincoln*.

12. Nothing great was ever achieved without enthusiasm.

13. The lowest ebb is the turn of the tide. *Henry Wadsworth Longfellow*.

ADVICE, CRITICISM

14. Advice is seldom welcome. Those who need it most like it least. *Samuel Johnson*.

15. Advice is seldom welcome; and those who want the most always like it the least. *Lord Chesterfield*.

16. Criticism is a study by which men grow important and formidable at very small expense. *Samuel Johnson*.

17. Often when we ask for advice we want approval.

18. Criticism takes the cumbersome mess of creative work and distills it into a fine essence. *Oscar Wilde*.

AGE

19. Growing old isn't half so bad when you think what is the alternative.

20. If only youth could invent and old age remember. Youth remembers but is mute. Old age cannot remember but invents.

21. The old believe everything; the middle-aged suspect everything; the young know everything. *Oscar Wilde*.

22. What find you better or more honourable than age? Take the pre-eminence of it in everything: in old friends, in

old wine, in an old pedigree. *Shakerley Marmion.*

23. Forty is the old age of youth, fifty is the youth of old age. *Victor Hugo.*

24. It is better to wear out than to rust out. *George Horne.*

25. Hardly any girl reaches the age of twenty-five without being asked to marry at least twice – once by her mother and once by her father.

26. A man is young so long as he looks.

ANTAGONISM, ADVERSITY, BIGOTRY

27. Always forgive your enemies, nothing annoys them so much. *Oscar Wilde.*

28. Civilization is only a slow process of getting rid of our prejudices.

29. Love, friendship, respect do not unite people as much as a common hatred of something. *Chekov.*

30. There is no good arguing with the inevitable. The only argument available with an East wind is to put on your overcoat. *J. R. Lowell.*

31. When men are full of envy they disparage everything, whether it is good or bad.

32. Adversity is the only diet that will reduce a fat head.

BACHELOR

33. All reformers are bachelors. *George Moore.*

34. A bachelor is a man who gets all the credit for what he does.

35. Not all men are fools; some are bachelors.

36. When a bachelor is pacing a room at midnight with a 'baby' in his arms, he is dancing.

BEHAVIOUR, CHARACTER

37. I count him braver who overcomes his desires than him who conquers his enemies; for the hardest victory is the victory over self.

38. Imitation is the sincerest form of flattery. *C. C. Colton.*

39. Behaviour is a mirror in which everyone shows his image. *Goethe*.

40. Selfishness is not living as one wishes to live; it is asking others to live as one wishes to live. And unselfishness is letting other people's lives alone, not interfering with them. Selfishness always aims at creating around it an absolute uniformity of type. Unselfishness recognizes infinite variety of type as a delightful thing, acquiesces in it, enjoys it. *Oscar Wilde*.

41. When men speak ill of thee, so live that no one will believe them. *Plato*.

42. An injury is much sooner forgotten than an insult. *Lord Chesterfield*.

43. A pig ought not to be blamed for being a pig but a man ought.

44. There is, however, a limit at which forbearance ceases to be a virtue. *Edmund Burke*.

45. Bright eyes are said to indicate curiosity – so do black eyes.

46. I'm only a beer-teetotaller, not a champagne tee-totaller. *G. Bernard Shaw*.

47. The measure of a man's real character is what he would do if he knew he would never be found out. *Thomas B. Macaulay*.

BUSINESS, WORK, BOSS

48. A boss is the man who is early when you are late and late when you are early.

49. Good salesmanship consists in selling goods that won't come back to customers who will.

50. With all these new office systems and business management methods who's going to do the work?

51. Those who complain that the boss is dumb would be out of a job if he were any smarter.

52. I like work; it fascinates me. I can sit and look at it for hours. I love to keep it by me; the idea of getting rid of it nearly breaks my heart. *Jerome K. Jerome*.

53. Too many people think they can push themselves forward by patting themselves on the back.

54. A dinner lubricates business. *Lord Stowell.*

55. The reasonable man adapts himself to the world; the unreasonable one persists in trying to adapt the world to himself. Therefore all progress depends on the unreasonable man. *G. Bernard Shaw.*

56. There are three kinds of lies: lies, damned lies and statistics. *Benjamin Disraeli.*

57. When a stupid man is doing something he is ashamed of he always declares it is his duty.

CHARITY

58. It is not enough to help the feeble up, but to support him after. *Shakespeare.*

59. In faith and hope the world will disagree, But all mankind's concern is charity. *Alexander Pope.*

60. Charity shall cover the multitude of sins. *1. Peter 2. v. 17.*

61. The living need charity more than the dead. *George Arnold.*

62. A rummage sale is where you buy stuff from somebody else's attic to store in your own.

COMMITTEE

63. A committee is a group of people who keep minutes and waste hours.

64. The best committee is a committee of one.

COURAGE, DESPAIR

65. Don't despair when you get spells of despondency. The sun has a sinking spell every night but it rises again all right the next morning.

65a. Many would be cowards if they had courage enough.

COURTS, POLICE, PRISONERS

66. Juvenile delinquents: other people's children.

67. It is just as well that justice is blind; she might not like some of the things done in her name if she could see them.

68. Stone walls do not a prison make,
   Nor iron bars a cage. *Richard Lovelace.*

69. Court: a place where they lock up juries and let out prisoners on bail.

70. Justice discards party, friendship, kindred and is always, therefore, represented as blind. *Joseph Addison.*

71. Justice pleaseth few in their own house.

72. The best prison built is but a monument to neglected youth.

73. In the course of justice none of us should see salvation. *Shakespeare.*

74. Justice is always violent to the offending, for every man is innocent in his own eyes. *Daniel Defoe.*

75. Store detective: Counter spy.

76. Ignorance of the law excuses no man; not that all men know the law but because 'tis an excuse every man will plead and no man can tell how to refute him. *John Selden.*

77. Care should be taken that the punishment does not exceed the guilt; and also that some men do not suffer for offences for which others are not even indicted. *Cicero.*

78. Every sin brings its punishment with it.

79. Corporal punishment falls on men more heavily than the most weighty pecuniary penalty. *Seneca.*

80. It is safer that a bad man should not be accused than that he should be acquitted.

DIET, FOOD, EATING

81. Obesity: Living beyond one's seams.

81a. An adult is someone who has stopped growing, except around the middle.

82. Reducing: wishful shrinking.

82a. Cauliflower is nothing but cabbage with a college education. *Mark Twain.*

83. Brussels-sprouts: a mouth-sized cabbage.

DOCTORING

83a. God heals, the doctor takes the fee. *Benjamin Franklin.*

EDUCATION

84. Education does not mean teaching people to know what they do not know; it means teaching them to behave as they do not behave. *John Ruskin.*

85. Education has for its object the formation of character. *Herbert Spencer.*

85a. Educational relations make the strongest tie. *Cecil John Rhodes.*

86. It is better neither to be able to read nor write than to be able to do nothing else. *W. Hazlitt.*

86a. Self-knowledge is the source of all philosophy.

87. If you can't spell the words in the first place how do they expect us to find them in a dictionary?

87a. 'What is the use of a book?' thought Alice, 'without pictures or conversations?' *Lewis Carroll.*

88. Examinations are formidable even to the best prepared, for the greatest fool may ask more than the wisest can answer. *C. C. Colton.*

88a. Life isn't all beer and skittles; but beer and skittles or something better of the same sort, must have formed a good part of every Englishman's education. *Thomas Hughes. Tom Brown's Schooldays.*

EXAMPLE

89. Everyone has some useful purpose in life – if only to serve as a horrible example.

90. An old man gives good advice in order to console himself for no longer being in a condition to set a bad example. *La Rochefoucauld.*

FINANCE, CREDIT, DEBTS.

91. Men do not realize how great a revenue economy is. *Cicero.*

92. When God gave man words to conceal thoughts, He gave him too, figures to conceal facts. *Anonymous*.

93. A debt is the only thing that doesn't become smaller when it is contracted.

94. A rolling stone gathers no moss but it gains a fine polish.

95. Debts are the certain outcome of an uncertain income.

FATHER, MOTHER, CHILDREN, ADOLESCENTS

96. A happy family is like a game of cricket with father bowling, mother wicket-keeping, the children fielding and all taking turns at the batting.

97. All happy families resemble one another; every unhappy family is unhappy in its own way.

98. Accidents will happen in the best regulated families.

99. Every dog is a lion at home.

100. A boy is a noise with dirt on it.

101. It is a wise child that knows his own father.

102. He that hath wife and children hath given hostages to fortune; for they are impediments to great enterprises either of virtue or mischief. *Francis Bacon*.

103. Home is the girl's prison and the woman's workhouse. *G. B. Shaw*.

104. 'Tis ever common that men are merriest when they are from home. *Shakespeare*.

105. Children who have grown up without the care of two parents, whether by reason of death or divorce usually face the world with less assurance than others.

106. Where there's a will, there are relatives.

107. It is a wise father that knows his own son. *Shakespeare*.

108. Adolescence is that time in a boy's life when he refuses to believe that one day he'll be a cabbage like his father.

FRIENDS, FRIENDSHIP

109. Great men taken up in any way are profitable friends. *Thomas Carlyle.*

110. Old friends are best. King James used to call for his old shoes; they were easiest for his feet. *John Selden.*

111. A man, sir, should keep his friendship in constant repair. *Samuel Johnson.*

112. Animals are such agreeable friends – they ask no questions, they pass no criticisms. *George Eliot.*

113. True friendship is like sound health, the value of it is seldom known until it is lost. *C.C. Colton.*

114. The only reward of virtue is virtue; the only way to have a friend is to be one. *R. Waldo Emerson.*

HAPPINESS

115. A life-time of happiness! No man could bear it; it would be hell on earth. *G. Bernard Shaw.*

116. Action may not always bring happiness; but there is no happiness without action.

117. There is nothing which has yet been contrived by man, by which so much happiness is produced as by a good tavern or inn. *Samuel Johnson.*

118. We have no more right to consume happiness without producing it than to consume wealth without producing it. *G. Bernard Shaw.*

HUMANITY

119. Life is like playing a violin solo and learning the instrument as one goes on. *Samuel Butler.*

120. Be virtuous and you will be vicious. *Samuel Butler.*

121. Conscience is thoroughly well-bred and soon leaves off talking to those who don't wish to hear it. *Samuel Butler.*

122. It is wise to lend a borrower half what he asks. If you give him all he will regret that he did not ask for more.

123. Ideas have to be refashioned in every epoch in a form that suits the intellectual habits of that epoch. To Moses the laws of hygiene had to be divine ordinances; to the modern

man moral laws have to be medical ordinances. Yet the laws themselves change but little and slowly. *André Maurois.*

124. The end of the human race will be that it will eventually die of civilization. *Ralph Waldo Emerson.*

125. As the French say, there are three sexes – men, women and clergymen. *Sydney Smith.*

126. The world is a comedy to those that think, a tragedy to those that feel. *Horace Walpole.*

127. The only way to get rid of a temptation is to yield to it. *Oscar Wilde.*

129. There is no more mean, stupid, dastardly, pitiful, selfish, spiteful, envious, ungrateful animal than the public. It is the greatest of cowards, for it is afraid of itself. *Wm. Hazlitt.*

130. The human species, according to the best theory I can form of it, is composed of two distinct races, the men who borrow and the men who lend. *Charles Lamb.*

131. All the world is queer save thee and me, and even thou are a little queer. *Robert Owen.*

132. He bade me observe it, and I should always find, that the calamities of life were shared among the upper and lower part of mankind; but that the middle station had the fewest disasters. *Daniel Defoe.*

133. There are two things to aim at in life; first to get what you want; and after that to enjoy it. Only the wisest of mankind achieve the second. *Logan Pearsall Smith.*

134. Life is one long process of getting tired. *Samuel Butler.*

135. God made the country, and man made the town. *W. Cowper.*

HUSBAND, MEN

136. Definition of luxury: Anything a husband needs.

137. Never trust the man who has reason to suspect that you know he has injured you. *Henry Fielding.*

138. Men are but children of a larger growth. *John Dryden.*

139. A husband is a man who has lost his liberty in the pursuit of happiness.

140. When the husband drinks to the wife, all would be well; when the wife drinks to the husband, all is well.

141. Imagination is something that stays up with a woman when her husband is late coming home.

142. The calmest husbands make the stormiest wives.

143. Girls want nothing but husbands, and when they have them they want everything.

144. A good wife makes a good husband.

145. A husband is what is left of a sweetheart after the nerve has been killed.

146. There is really no difference between an old maid and a married woman. The old maid is always looking for a husband and so is the married woman.

147. Men are not to be measured by inches.

148. 'Tis all a Chequer-board of Nights and Days
   Where Destiny with Men for Pieces plays;
      Hither and thither moves and mates and slays,
      And one by one back in the Closet lays.

Omar Khayyam.

149. I've studied men from topsy-turvy
   Close, and I reckon, rather true
Some are fine fellows; some right scurvy,
   Most a dash between the two.

George Meredith.

150. The history of the world is but the biography of great men. *Thomas Carlyle.*

151. Men are like fish; neither would get into trouble if they kept their mouths shut.

152. All men think all men mortal but themselves. *Edward Young.*

SAINTLINESS, INTEGRITY, TRUTH

153. If one tells the truth, one is sure, sooner or later to be found out.

154. Truth is elastic. Don't stretch it unless you want it to

fly back and sting you.

155. Face to face the truth comes out.

156. Truth finds enemies where it makes none.

157. Speak the truth sparingly unless you want to live the life of a hermit.

158. Truth and roses have thorns about them.

159. The only time a fisherman tells the truth is when he calls another fisherman a liar.

160. Children and fools speak the truth.

161. The only difference between the saint and the sinner is that every saint has a past and every sinner has a future. *Oscar Wilde*.

162. There is more hope for a self-confessed sinner than there is for a self-conceived saint.

163. Knowledge without integrity is dangerous and dreadful. *Samuel Johnson*.

164. God hath made man upright; but they have sought out many inventions. *Ecclesiastes, i, 2*.

LOVE, COURTING, WEDDING

165. The bonds of matrimony are worthless unless the interest is kept up.

166. The reason so few marriages are happy, is, because young ladies spend their time in making nets, not in making cages.

167. People wouldn't get divorced for such trivial reasons if they didn't get married for such trivial reasons.

168. In marriage a man becomes slack and selfish, and undergoes a fatty degeneration of his moral being. *R. L. Stevenson*.

169. To marry is to domesticate the Recording Angel. Once you are married, there is nothing left for you, not even suicide, but to be good. *R. L. Stevenson*.

170. By all means marry. If you get a good wife, you will become very happy; if you get a bad one, you will become a philosopher – and that is good for every man. *Socrates*.

171. Woman begins by resisting men's advances and ends

by blocking his retreat. *Oscar Wilde*.

172. A lover without indiscretion is no lover at all. *Thomas Hardy*.

173. Love is like the measles – all the worse when it comes late in life. *Douglas William Jerrold*.

174. We always believe our first love is our last and our last love our first. *G. J. Whyte-Melville*.

175. A house-warming is the last call for wedding presents.

176. Too many mothers-in-law forget they were once daughters-in-law.

POLITICS

177. All governments are party governments. *Edmund Burke*.

178. There are five main parties in Great Britain:
The Conservative Party
The Labour Party
The Social Democratic Party
The Liberal Party and The Cocktail Party.

179. The minds of some of our own statesmen like the pupil of the human eye, contract themselves the more, the stronger light there is shed upon them. *Thomas More*.

180. When a politician comes to the parting of the ways, he goes both ways.

181. I'm not a politician and my other habits are good. *Artemus Ward*.

182. Politicians neither love nor hate. *William Drummond*.

183. Some people fall for everything and stand for nothing.

184. Kings will be tyrants from policy when subjects are rebels from principle. *Edmund Burke*.

PUBLIC SPEAKING, CHAIRMAN

185. The interpretation of a speech is like the compound fracture of an idea. *Woodrow Wilson*.

186. Some people speak from experience. Others – from experience – don't speak.

187. An after-dinner speaker is a man who rises to the occasion and then stands too long.

188. In public speaking, if you don't strike oil in five minutes stop boring.

189. The tongue is but three inches long but it can kill a man six foot tall.

190. Blessed is the man who having nothing to say, abstains from giving us wordy evidence of the fact. *George Eliot.*

191. One of the reasons there are so few really good public speakers is that there are so few good thinkers in private.

192. The function of a chairman in relation to a speaker is like that of a kerchief to the dancer: it calls attention to the subject, but makes no attempt to cover it.

193. After that wonderful introduction by the Chairman I can't wait, until I hear what I have to say.

194. Swans sing before they die; 'twere no bad thing should certain persons die before they sing. *Samuel T. Coleridge.*

RESOURCEFULNESS, INGENUITY

195. Necessity is the mother of invention.

SECRET

196. Stolen waters are sweet, and bread eaten in secret is pleasant. *Proverbs ix, 17.*

197. He that tells a secret is another's servant.

198. A secret is something which is hushed about from place to place.

199. He that hath a secret should not only hide it, but hide that he has it to hide. *Thomas Carlyle.*

200. Every daisy in the dell knows my secret,
     knows it well,
    But yet I dare not tell, sweet Marie.
Cy. Warman.

201. It's a great kindness to trust people with a secret. They feel so important while telling it. *Robert Quillen*.

202. Time and chance reveal all secrets.

203. Three are too many to keep a secret, and too many to be merry.

204. If you would know secrets look for them in grief and pleasures.

SERVICES, COUNTRY

205. When bad men combine, the good must associate, else they will fall, one by one, an unpitied sacrifice in a contemptible struggle. *Edmund Burke*.

206. Our Country! In her intercourse with foreign nations, may she be always in the right; but our country, right or wrong. *Stephen Decatur*.

> *U.S. Naval Commander, in a toast given at Norfolk, Virginia, April 1816.*

207. As long as war is regarded as wicked, it will always have its fascination. When it is looked upon as vulgar, it will cease to be popular. *Oscar Wilde*.

208. Learn to speak imperially! *Joseph Chamberlain*.

209. The condition upon which God hath given liberty to man is eternal vigilance. *John Philpot Curran*.

SMOKING

210. Tobacco, divine, rare, super-excellent tobacco, which goes far beyond all their panaceas, potable gold and philosopher's stones, a sovereign remedy to all diseases. *Robert Burton, 17th century clergyman and author*.

211. But as it is commonly abused by most men, which take it as tinkers do to ale, 'tis a plague, a mischief, a violent purger of goods, lands, health, hellish, devilish and damned tobacco, the ruin and overthrow of body and soul. *Ditto!*

SOCIETY, COMPANY

212. Social success is an infinite capacity for being bored.

213. Be wiser than other people if you can, but do not tell

them so. *Lord Chesterfield.*

214. When you are in company, talk often, but not long; in that case if you do not please, at least you are sure not to tire your hearers. *Lord Chesterfield.*

215. Success is important in one's own circle. Failure is to be thwarted or disgraced outside one's private circle or inside one's professional association.

216. I have no relish for the country; it is a kind of healthy grave. *Sydney Smith.*

SPORT

217. A golfer has one advantage over a fisherman. He doesn't have to produce anything to prove his story.

218. In sports and journeys men are known.

TOASTS

219. Here's to wives and sweethearts – may they never meet.

220. I wish you health – a little wealth
　　　And a happy home with freedom
　　And may you always have true friends
　　　But never have cause to need them.

WOMEN, WIFE

221. Apologize to a man if you're wrong but to a woman even if you're right.

222. Women are much more like each other than men; they have in truth but two passions, vanity and love. *Lord Chesterfield.*

223. I have always thought that every woman should marry and no man. *Disraeli.*

224. Women, priests and poultry never have enough.

225. When I speak of men, I speak of them as embracing women.

226. All women become like their mothers – that is their tragedy. No man does, that is his. *Oscar Wilde.*

227. Women's styles may change; but their designs

remain the same. *Oscar Wilde.*

228. Women are meant to be loved, not understood. *Oscar Wilde.*

229. A smart man is one who has never let a woman pin anything on him since he was a baby.

230. Women are saints in church, angels in the street, devils in the kitchen and apes in bed.

231. One should never trust a woman who tells one her real age. A woman who would tell one that would tell one anything.

232. I expect that woman will be the last thing civilized by man. *George Meredith.*

233. But what is woman? – only one of Nature's agreeable blunders.

234. Trade secret: What housewives do.

TRAGEDY

235. There are two tragedies in life. One is not to get your heart's desire, the other is to get it. *G. Bernard Shaw.*

YOUTH

236. Youth is a blunder; manhood a struggle; old age a regret. *Disraeli.*

237. Home-keeping youths have ever homely wits. *Shakespeare.*

238. Youth and white paper take any impression.

239. No young man believes he shall ever die. *Wm. Hazlitt.*

240. Youth and age will never agree.

241. If youth knew what age would crave, it would both get and save.

242. You are only young once, but you can stay immature indefinitely.

STORIES AND ANECDOTES

243. The Sunday School teacher who had been telling his class the story of Jonah and the whale finished by asking them what lesson they thought the story taught.

One little boy put up his hand. 'Please, sir,' he piped, 'that you can't keep a good man down.'

244. A man who had been boasting of his achievements for what seemed hours at last concluded with: 'I'm a self-made man! That's what I am, a self-made man!'

One of the company, stifling a yawn observed in a bored voice: 'Really, old man! Then you gave up work too soon!'

245. 'Success changes people,' observed the business tycoon smiling sardonically. 'I'm now said to be eccentric, not impolite; witty not infernally rude!'

246. Two young ladies were talking. One said to the other: 'My husband tricked me into marrying him. Before we got engaged he said he was a multi-millionaire.'

The other one replied: 'But he *is* a multi-millionaire isn't he?'

'Yes, but he also said he was 84 and in poor health. But I have just found out that he is only 75 and in perfect condition.'

247. Two high-minded young students were visiting the Church of Ara Coeli, hoping to recapture the atmosphere in which Gibbon was inspired to start his history of the Decline and Fall of the Roman Empire when three Germans walked in. They kept their hats on and continued smoking cigars as they went around the Church in which they even spat. The

two friends left the Church in disgust at such behaviour. At the door one remarked: 'Well, we didn't succeed in seeing much of the past.' 'No,' said his friend bitterly, 'but we have seen quite a lot of the future.'

CRITICISM

248. When an author read the review of his new book he was so angry that he picked up a riding crop and rushed to the house of the critic. There, having been shown into the sitting-room by a servant, he brandished his whip at the reviewer and demanded satisfaction.

The critic who could be extremely affable when he pleased, invited him to sit down, and remarking on how cold the day was proceeded to poke the fire, leaving the poker in the grate.

For five minutes he talked pleasantly to the author, then the conversation became hostile. The author began to wave his whip again, but before he had a chance to use it the critic snatched the poker, which was now red hot, from the fire, and chased him out of his house.

AGE

249. A man's not old when his hair turns grey,
     A man's not old when his teeth decay,
   But a man's getting near his last long sleep
     When his mind makes appointments
   Which his body can't keep.

250. The fuss you made of that minx,' complained the middle-aged wife to her husband. 'Are you already in your second childhood?'

'Not yet,' the husband's eyes continued to twinkle. 'But perhaps I'm just starting on my second adolescence!'

AMERICA

251. A father was asking his son what he had learnt at school that day. .

'All about George Washington,' answered his son.

'And what makes him stand out among all the other famous Americans?' asked the father.

'He was the one who never told a lie.'

252. Fourscore and seven years ago our fathers brought forth on this continent a new nation conceived in liberty and dedicated to the proposition that all men are created equal. Now we are engaged in a great civil war, testing whether that nation or any nation so conceived and so dedicated, can long endure.

We are met on a great battlefield of that war. We have come to dedicate a portion of that field as a final resting place of those who here gave their lives that that nation might live. It is altogether fitting and proper that we should do this. But in a large sense, we cannot dedicate, we cannot consecrate, we cannot hallow, this ground. The brave men, living and dead who struggled here have consecrated it far above our poor power to add or detract.

The world will little note nor long remember what we say here, but it can never forget what they did here. It is for us, the living, rather to be dedicated here to the unfinished work which they who fought here have thus far so nobly advanced.

It is rather for us to be here dedicated to the great task remaining before us – that from these honoured dead we take increased devotion to that cause for which they gave the last full measure of devotion; that we here highly resolve that these dead shall not have died in vain, that this nation, under God, shall have a new birth of freedom, and that government of the people, by the people, for the people, shall not perish from the Earth. *Abraham Lincoln. Gettysburg, 19th November 1863.*

ANTAGONISM, ADVERSITY, BIGOTRY

253. A Lancashireman entered a Liverpool public house with a crocodile on a lead.

'Do you serve Yorkshiremen here?' he asked.

The barman gulped and stammered: 'Y . . . yes.'

'Well,' said the Lancashireman, 'a pint of bitter for me and two Yorkshiremen for my crocodile.'

BEHAVIOUR, CHARACTER

254. We are in a desperate state, feet frozen, etc. No fuel and a long way from food, but it would do your heart good to be in our tent to hear our songs and the cheery conversation. *Robert Falcon Scott. Farewell letter to Sir J. M. Barrie.*

255. An old lady crippled with rheumatism was about to step on to a bus when a young man who was standing beside her asked if he might help her. She smiled but shook her head as she said, 'No, thank you. I'd best manage on my own. You see if I get helped today, I'll want it again tomorrow.'

256. Milton, who in his Cambridge days was known as 'the Lady of Christ's College' and whom Tennyson called 'The Organ Voice of England' could be anything but sweet and gentle when opposed. In a pamphlet he referred to a contemporary lawyer who had criticized his views on divorce as a beast, a cockbrained solicitor, a pork who never read any philosophy, a boar in a vineyard, a snout in pickle, an unswilled hogshead, a mere and arrant pettifogger, a tradesman of the law whose best ware is only gibberish, an unbuttoned fellow, a serving-man and solicitor compounded into one mongrel, an apostate scarecrow, a vagabond and ignoramus, a beetle, a horsefly, a broken ass ...

BUSINESS, BOSS, WORK

257. A business consultant came to give a lecture to the executive officers of a large company on how great economies had been made by considering anew the methods they employed. He started by putting a large white sheet of paper on the wall. In the middle of it he drew a small black spot.

'What do you see?' he asked an executive officer.

'A black spot,' answered the executive officer.

He asked every man in the room the same question and in

every case got the same reply: 'A black spot!'

'Quite right,' he observed, 'there is a black spot there but none of you has mentioned the large white sheet. And that will be the subject of my lecture.'

258. A man who was applying for a job as a chauffeur was being interviewed by the wife of the house.

'We call all our servants by their surnames,' she told him. 'What's yours?'

'I think you'd better call me John,' answered the handsome young man.

'I'm sorry!' The wife shook her head. 'If you're not willing to be called by your surname we can't employ you.'

'Oh, I'm willing, all right,' smiled the applicant, 'but I don't think you'd like to use it.'

'Why not?' demanded the wife expecting to hear a name which had made the headlines in connection with something scandalous.

'Darling, ma'am; John Darling.'

259. A girl who was being interviewed for a job was asked if she had any special qualifications or abilities.

'Oh, yes,' she replied, 'I've won prizes for crosswords and limericks.'

'That's very good,' smiled the employer, 'but we want someone who is clever during office hours.'

The girl sat up: 'But I did them during office hours.'

260. 'Did you notice how Joan purposely stumbled so that the boss's son caught her?' asked one salesgirl of another.

'Yes.' retorted her friend, 'I'd call it a business trip.'

261. The Author's Prayer: 'Lord give us this day our daily idea, and forgive us what we thought yesterday.'

262. A young man who had been a shop-assistant got very fed up with trying to please all sorts of awkward customers so he resigned and joined a police force.

Six months later he met one of the salesgirls who had worked with him in the shop. 'How do you like your new job?' she asked.

'Fine!' He smiled broadly: 'In the force the customer is always wrong.'

263. 'One way to solve the unemployment problem,' said the club wag, 'is to put all the men on one island and all the women on another. That would soon make them busy.'

'Doing what?' asked a listener.

'Boat-building!'

264. The woman who had just been shown the photograph which an exclusive studio had taken of her turned to the photographer. 'Good heavens!' she exclaimed frowning. 'Am I really like that?'

The long-haired photographer smiled blandly: 'Madam the answer is in the "negative".'

265. Wife: 'Why did the foreman sack you?'

Husband: 'Well, you know what foremen are? How they stand around while the men work.'

Wife: 'Yes, but what has that got to do with it?'

Husband: 'Well, this one was jealous. People used to think I was the foreman.'

266. A man staying at an English hotel walked into the cocktail bar after hours and asked for a drink.

'Are you a guest, sir?' asked the good-looking young barman.

'Guest? Good heavens, no, I'm paying.'

267. Adam and Eve did not take to wearing fig leaves out of modesty, but because they were Jews and wanted to start the clothing trade.

268. In the arithmetic lesson the teacher asked the class: 'If toffees cost a pound a ½ kilogram, how much would I get for 100p?'

One little boy put up his hand at once.

'Yes, Billy?' said the teacher.

Billy frowned, 'Please miss, a little less than half a kilogram.

The teacher shook her head, 'That's not right, Billy'.

'I know, miss, but they all do it!'

269. An old gentleman went into a shoe shop and asked

for a pair of shoes. The assistant produced a pair which the old gentleman tried. They fitted perfectly, but the old gentleman was not satisfied. 'Their quality,' he observed, 'is not very good, is it? They won't last very long will they?'

The young shop-assistant was annoyed. 'How old are you, Sir?' he asked.

'Eighty-two,' answered the old gentleman.

'Well,' said the young man, 'begging your pardon, Sir, they'll probably last you long enough.'

The old gentleman shook his head and said: 'Statistics, you know, prove that fewer people die at my age than almost any other.'

270. Robinson Crusoe, so to speak,
    Began the forty hour week,
He lived on an island, neat and tidy,
    And all his work was done by Friday.

CHARITY

271. Two lady social workers who were collecting for a highly deserving local charity called on a well-known miser. They spent half an hour telling him about the excellent work the charity did and its great need. But all they got out of him was an insulting refusal.

As they shook the dust of his house off their feet the elder of the two ladies observed: 'And to think that old skinflint has money to burn.'

Her companion smiled thinly: 'Yes, what's more that's what would happen to it if he could take it with him.'

272. At a charity ball the celebrity was doing a duty dance with a silly woman who simpered: 'Do tell me, you wonderful man, why did you ask me of all people to dance with you?'

The celebrity looked at her distastefully: 'It's a charity dance, isn't it?'

273. What a pity people who complain about others 'violating the decencies of nature' do not consider what they are saying. A little charity in their attitude would often be

more helpful and constructive. The phrase comes all too often from the bench in Courts of Law where to put it mildly it would be imprudent for the unfortunate to whom it is addressed to reply suitably.

Actually, a Court of Law is the last place where anyone should complain about the decencies of nature. When has nature ever been decent by the standards of any of them? Breathing is about the only natural process one may perform in our courts without causing a Breach of the Peace, and indeed in polite circles breathing is indecent when it is not silent.

274. At a Charity Concert the Chairman at the end of his speech appealing for funds said: 'Stand up those who will donate ten pounds.'

No one stood up.

The Chairman looked around the audience hopefully for a few minutes then took a card from his pocket which he passed to the leader of the orchestra who nodded and quickly passed it to his orchestra to read.

On the card was written: 'When I ask them to stand up for £5, play the National Anthem.'

275. At the end of a church service in Australia the Vicar found the Churchwarden, who had been counting the collection, almost in tears. He asked him what was wrong and was told: 'Someone has only put 2 cents on the collecting plate!'

The Vicar looked at the pile of notes and silver alongside the solitary two-cent piece and smiled indulgently, 'Don't take it too hard. Everybody else has given pretty well.'

'It's not that,' moaned the Churchwarden. 'Don't you see there was someone in the congregation straight from the Old Country and I missed him!'

276. A wealthy lady was leaving a hotel at which she had been attending an exclusive and expensive Charity Ball. As she was about to enter her limousine a beggar sidled up to her. 'Ma'am,' he pleaded, 'please spare a starving man a few pence.'

At once she recoiled. 'Is there no end to what you people expect?' she retorted. 'I've been dancing my feet off for you all night and already you want more money!'

277. A friend of mine was telling me about how he was out walking one Sunday evening when he saw a youth, who was playing with a friend on the parapet of a bridge, suddenly fall into the river beneath. At once the youth was in difficulties. No one else seemed able to do anything, so my friend dived in and saved him.

He got no thanks from the youth or his friends and had to walk home, squelching at every step, and a spectacle in dripping clothes.

As a result he got a chill and had to stay in bed for a couple of days. His suit will never be the same and his wristwatch is ruined.

He is still wondering whether this was God's reward for virtue or whether the trouble came because he was not in church that Sunday evening attending evensong.

COURTS

278. The jury had been out since just after the lunch break trying to decide whether the man was guilty or not and they were still fifty/fifty for Guilty/Not-Guilty. Neither side could persuade even one of the other to change his mind, and it was a case of either a majority opinion or spending the night miserably away from home and returning the following day to try again.

The hours had passed slowly, but it was now almost five and the court janitor knocked at the door to ask if they would want dinner or not.

'We will,' said the foreman wearily 'order six dinners and six bales of hay.'

279. A young married couple received by post two tickets for a popular musical. Accompanying them was a card. On it was written: 'Guess who from?'

All day they pondered who the kind person was. In the evening they went to the show.

When they returned to their home they found that their home had been burgled and all their wedding presents and other valuables stolen. On the mantelpiece there was a card similar to that which had accompanied the tickets to the theatre. On it was written: 'Now you know who from.'

280. It had been a long and tiring case during which there had been a great deal of wrangling between counsel. But at last it was over and the jury had returned a verdict of guilty.

'You may,' said the judge to the prisoner, 'think from all the talking you have heard during the last two days that the legal profession is composed of gentlemen who have far too much to say. Indeed, even some of Her Majesty's judges are said to be men of many words and short sentences.

'You will be sorry to hear that I am not one of these. I am a man of few words and long sentences. You will go to prison for seven years.'

281. The charges before the Court were for Common Assault and a Breach of the Peace, and in each case there were cross-summonses all of which had been taken out by the defendants, one against the other.

When the Magistrate had listened to the evidence and what the solicitors had to say, he enquired, mildly: 'Couldn't this have been settled out of Court?'

Patrick, who still had traces of a black-eye, answered at once, 'Sure, Sir, and it could, Your Worship, an' that's what Mick and me was trying to do, but our misusses came along. And to be sure, after that they had to go and get legal advice!'

282. The penitent had just confessed to stealing a duck and the priest had told him that it was very wrong.

'Won't you have it, Father?' suggested the penitent.

'I will do nothing of the kind!' retorted the priest. 'I don't want stolen property. Go and return it to the man from whom you stole it.'

'But I have offered it to him and he refused it!' said the man.

'In that event you may keep it yourself.'

'Thank you, Father,' fawned the penitent.

That evening when the priest got home his house-keeper told him that one of his ducks was missing.

283. The policeman was giving the court his evidence.

'It was dark, Your Worship,' he said 'the car was leaving the golf club and had no lights, so I stopped it, and pointed out to the driver the offence he was committing.'

'He, sir, said he had exceptional eyesight and didn't need lights. Then I asked for his driving licence,' and the officer consulted his notebook. 'He said, "I never had one".'

'When I asked him to produce his certificate of insurance, he said he didn't need one as he never had accidents. Then, sir, he explained he hadn't a Road Fund Licence because he didn't use the car much. Then his wife intervened. She, sir said, "Take no notice of him, he's drunk!"'

284. The Magistrate was listening to charges arising as a result of a car accident. 'How far were you from where the cars collided?' he asked a witness who had been a bystander when the accident occurred.

'Nineteen foot five and a half inches!' answered the cantankerous old man.

The Magistrate raised his eyebrows. 'Did you measure it?'

'I did,' answered the old man coldly. 'I expected some fool would ask me for it!'

WAITER

285. A customer had already waited twenty minutes for the fish which he had ordered when the waiter returned to him to say that his fish would be another five minutes.

He waited another quarter of an hour then he summoned the waiter again. 'Tell me,' he said, 'what kind of bait are you using?'

WEIGHT

286. A plump woman climbed off the weighing machine, a frown on her face. As she consulted the Height/Weight Chart above it however, she began to smile. 'Do you know,' she said presently, 'I'm four inches too short!'

DENTISTS

287. McTavish met his friend McIntyre on the street one day. 'I've just seen your Andrew,' he said. 'You told me he was studying to be an ear-specialist. He just told me now he's going to be a dentist. How's he changed his mind?'

'I'm not too sure, Sandy,' answered McIntyre. 'All I know is I told him folk have 32 teeth but only two ears.'

DOCTORS

288. 'Doctor,' began the patient, 'Isn't it out of your way to come here to me?'

'Not terribly,' smiled the doctor. 'You see I've another patient fairly close to you and I've always believed it's a good thing when you can kill two birds with one stone.'

289. 'Have you been to see a doctor before me?' asked a doctor irritably of a patient who had neglected his condition.

'No, sir,' said the patient.

'You're sure you've had no other medical advice?'

'Well, sir, I did go to the chemist,' admitted the man.

The doctor groaned and shook his head despairingly. 'Don't you know a chemist knows nothing about diagnosis?' he asked, then shrugged contemptuously. 'Anyhow what crackpot advice did he give you?'

'He told me to come and see you, sir!'

290. The telephone has curative properties according to some asthma sufferers. Often when they try to get their doctor on the telephone they experience such exasperation over finding his number, being delayed in getting through to him, not hearing or properly understanding what he says, that it produces in them a flow of adrenalin almost as reviving as an injection.

Some passions are bad for asthma, but certainly not anger – it is excellent.

291. Two Irishwomen, who had not met for years, were talking about their husbands who were now dead.

'Mine died in a car crash,' said one. 'Did yours die a natural death?'

'By the saints, no,' retorted her friend, 'he had a doctor!'

292. The teacher had sent for the mother of one of her pupils. 'Mrs. Smith,' she said, 'I'm worried about your little girl. I'm afraid that she's psychologically confused. If she doesn't get treatment she'll develop into a problem child.'

'What makes you say that?' demanded the mother, alarmed.

'Well, when I asked her whether she was a boy or a girl she insisted she was a boy!'

The mother on her way home with her little girl asked her why she had told her teacher she was a little boy.

'Shucks,' retorted her daughter, 'when anyone asks me a silly question I always give a silly answer.'

DIPLOMACY

293. 'That boy of yours, the one who is in college,' said the man at the golf club to a friend, 'what's he preparing for?'

'Well, I really don't know,' replied the father, 'but from the way he works on me I think he'll be a diplomat.'

294. 'Television has done a great deal for my education,' observed the Vicar. 'Almost every time somebody turns it on I go into another room and read a book.'

295. Two students were discussing what to do with their evening. 'Let's toss a coin,' suggested one. 'Heads we go to the pictures. Tails to Helen and Joy's.'

'What happens if it stands on its edge?' asked his friend.

'Then we'll swot!'

296. 'Teacher,' asked the precocious small boy, 'can someone be punished for something he didn't do?'

'No, of course not,' said the teacher.

'Well, I haven't done my homework.'

'You lazy boy!' the teacher frowned: 'I wish I were your mother for a week!!'

'All right, Miss,' smiled the boy. 'I'll talk to Dad about it. Maybe he'll fix it!'

EXAMPLE OF NAÏVETÉ

297. Children have a charming way of veiling unpleasant

facts. A city boy taken to a farm recently and overhearing a conversation about taking a pig to the butcher remarked naïvely: 'What, kill the nice pig, that gives us such lovely bacon!'

FINANCE, CREDIT, DEBTS

298. 'There's one poster I'd like to see in every post office and on every pillar box,' said the weary business man who was having an unpleasant interview with his accountant.

'And what is that?' asked the accountant coldly.

'Post no bills!'

299. 'I'm sorry, but I can't pay my hire purchase instalments this week,' said the housewife.

The shopkeeper frowned. 'But that's what you said last week,' he complained.

'I know,' the woman smiled: 'And didn't I keep my promise?'

300. 'Above all,' said the consultant to a private patient, 'you mustn't worry. When a worry comes along just throw it on one side.'

'That's easier said than done,' answered the sick business man. 'But what would you say if I did that with your bill when it comes along?'

301. 'You are suffering from scarlet fever,' said the doctor to the man in bed, 'and it's extremely contagious.'

The man turned to his wife. 'Did you hear that?' he asked. 'If any of my creditors call tell them that at last I've got something to give them.'

302. In desperation the young man went to see his father. 'Dad,' he said, 'I lent Bill Smithers a hundred pounds and now he doesn't look at me even. What's worse he gave me no security. I haven't even got an I.O.U. from him!'

His father smiled at him hopefully. 'Perhaps things aren't as bad as they look,' he said. 'Write him a note asking for your two hundred pounds back.'

'But it's a hundred he owes me, not two hundred,' retorted the son.

His father shook his head despairingly: 'If you write saying he owes you two hundred he's bound to write back correcting you and saying he only owes you a hundred. Then you've got it in writing!'

FATHER, MOTHER, CHILDREN, ADOLESCENCE

303. When his father came home the boy's mother complained bitterly about their son's behaviour.

'You promised me you'd be a good boy, didn't you?' demanded the father heavily.

The boy nodded sullenly: 'Yes, Dad.'

'And I promised you a sound spanking if you weren't, didn't I?'

'Yes, Dad,' the boy smiled hopefully, 'But since I broke my promise, you needn't keep yours.'

304. 'Everybody in our house is some sort of animal,' mused Johnny to a friend. 'Mummy's a dear, Baby's a baa-lamb, Dad's an old goat and I'm the kid.'

305. Every night as he went to the local leaving her alone with the children her husband said: 'Good-bye, mother of four!'

For some time she had been dissatisfied with being left alone and had thought a good deal about what she could do to change this. One night as he left with his usual greeting of 'Good-bye, mother of four,' she replied pleasantly: 'Good-bye, father of two.'

'Good-bye, father of two!' he repeated to himself all the way to the pub.

That was the last night he went out on his own.

306. 'Have I told you about my grandchildren?' asked a woman of another whom she met at the Church Sewing Guild.

'No, dear,' smiled the other, 'and I'd like you to know that I appreciate it.'

307. A teacher who had been talking to her class about the variable weather we have in March asked her class: 'What comes in like a lion and goes out like a lamb?'

One little boy put up his hand. 'Please, miss' he said, 'Daddy!'

308. When the little boy came home from school he asked: 'Where's Daddy?'

His mother, who had just returned from the Court, replied: 'He's gone away. And if anyone asks you be sure to say for a fortnight – not fourteen days!'

309. 'Tommy,' said his mother, 'there were two pieces of cake in the larder this morning. How is it that there is only one there now?'

'Dunno, Mummy. It was so dark there I didn't see the other piece!'

310. 'Tell your wife not to worry because she's getting slightly deaf,' said the doctor. 'It's one of the things she can expect now she's getting on in years.'

The husband looked worried for a moment then said: 'Would you mind, Doctor, telling her that yourself?'

311. The boy rubbing his behind tenderly was complaining to his friend: 'You don't know where you are in our house. When I'm noisy they spank me and when I'm quiet they give me castor oil!'

312. The man and his wife had been quarrelling for some moments.

'I wish,' wailed the wife, 'I'd listened to my mother and never married you.'

The husband pricked up his ears: 'You're not saying your mother tried to prevent our marrying?' he demanded.

'I am!' she retorted.

'Heavens above!' He put his hand to his mouth in horror: 'How I've wronged that woman!!'

313. 'I can read you like a book,' said the irate father to his son.

'I wish you would,' returned the youth. 'You might then skip over what you don't like instead of lingering over it and carrying on as you do!'

FRIENDS, FRIENDSHIP

314. The occasion when friends and relations are persistently unreliable is when one departs this life. Frequently one's well-known wishes as to the disposal of one's body and funeral ceremony are not only ignored but flouted. It seems it is quite useless leaving instructions unless one tells executors beforehand that one is leaving them a legacy in his will which is held by one's lawyer along with instructions as to the disposal of one's body, and that the legacy will only be paid on condition that these instructions are carried out precisely.

315. A journalist was asked to lunch by the late Lord Beaverbrook at his flat. Before they went into the dining-room the great newspaperman asked his guest what wine he liked. 'Claret, please,' replied the journalist.

'An excellent choice,' remarked Lord Beaverbrook. But when they went in to lunch, which was an excellent meal, the wine served was hock. The journalist wondered why Lord Beaverbrook had asked him what wine he liked when clearly he had already made up his mind that they were going to drink hock, no matter what he said. He decided presently that it was an eccentricity of his host.

When he was leaving the flat, however, Lord Beaverbrook presented him with a parcel. When he got home he discovered it contained a bottle of splendid claret.

HUMANITY

316. Billy who had forgotten the birthday of one of his friends decided to write to him apologizing.

'I do hope you will forgive me,' he wrote, 'my mother says it would serve me jolly well right if you forgot my birthday next Saturday.'

317. A young man who was temporarily hard-up had to take his girl friend to supper at a restaurant. While she was in the cloak-room he had a confidential chat with the waiter who spoilt everything when presently he brought the menu to the two of them and said to the man: 'It's all right, sir. Like

you said, I've crossed out all the expensive dishes!'

318. The family had all been to church and were together again sitting down to lunch when Dad started complaining bitterly: 'No wonder the churches are nearly empty. The singing this morning was painful. And that chap who read the lessons – I couldn't hear half of what he was saying. But worst of all was the sermon – that was really terrible.'

Suddenly he noticed that his small son was smiling broadly.

'And what have you got to grin at?' he demanded indignantly.

'Well, Dad,' said the boy, 'I didn't think it was too bad a show for 10p!'

319. One day the Head-keeper at the Zoo was surprised to see an ape with a Bible in one hand and Darwin's *Origin of Species* in the other. He appeared to be reading from one and then the other.

The Head-keeper watched him for a while then asked him what he was doing.

'Well,' said the ape, looking from one book to the other, 'I am trying to decide whether I am my brother's keeper or whether the Keeper is my brother!'

320. 'These photographs!' frowned the customer on the pier, 'I'm sure they don't do me justice!!'

'Justice, madam?' repeated the seaside photographer. 'It's not justice you need but mercy!'

321. A Child's Prayer: 'Please God make the bad people good and the good people kind!'

322. A father hoping to keep his young son quiet pulled a page out of a magazine on which there was a map of the world. This he tore into several small pieces which he gave to the boy. 'There,' he said, 'go into the next room and put that jig-saw together.'

The boy left the room, but in five minutes returned with the job done and held together with sticky tape.

'How did you manage it?' demanded his father in astonishment.

'Well, Dad,' said the boy, 'I tried putting the world together for some time and found that I couldn't. But then I found that on the other side there was a picture of a man. So I stuck the picture of the man together, turned it round and found I'd put the world together again.'

And the moral of that story is that if you want to put the world together you should first put man together!

HUSBAND

323. The Judge adjourned the Married Woman's Separation case for a few moments. From his chambers he sent for the husband. When the husband was ushered into the room the Judge said to him: 'Your wife says that you keep her in a state of terror. Now forget for a moment that I'm a Judge, will you, and tell me confidentially how you manage it.'

324. 'I remember,' said the bachelor to an old friend who had been married some years, 'the time when you had plenty of clothes for every occasion.'

The husband smiled at him indulgently: 'I've still got a suit for every day of the week,' he said, 'and this is it!'

325. The husband who brags: 'I run things at home,' usually means the lawn mower, the sweeper, the washing-up machine and the errands.

326. A young bride went into a chemist's shop and said: 'I want a tonic which makes babies bigger and stronger, please.'

As the chemist gave her the bottle she drew him aside and whispered: 'Do I give it to my husband or do I take it?'

INSURANCE

327. Strong hands pushed out of the court the wheelchair in which sat the man who had just been awarded £500,000 damages for the injuries he had received in a motor car crash. In the corridor he encountered once again the private detective whom the insurance company employed.

'I'm going to watch you like a hawk' announced the private detective. 'Watch you wherever you go. Just in case you sometimes forget you're paralysed from the waist down.'

'I thought you would,' he said. 'And to save you a lot of bother I'll give you my itinerary. From here, I'm going to the Savoy Hotel, where I'll spend the night. Tomorrow I'm crossing over to Paris. There I'll spend the night at the Ritz. Then the following morning I'll travel on to Lourdes.' His smile grew: 'If you happen to be at Lourdes you'll witness one of the most successful miracles ever to take place there.'

SAINTLINESS, INTEGRITY, TRUTH

328. 'What happens to boys who tell lies?' asked Tommy's new uncle.

'They travel cheaper on the buses!' was the prompt reply.

329. Years ago two brothers were convicted of sheep-stealing. Part of their punishment was that they be branded on the forehead with the letters: 'S T' which meant Sheep-Thief.

One of them, unable to stand the disgrace, afterwards fled the country. But because people were always asking him about his branding wherever he went he found no comfort anywhere. Like Cain he became a wanderer until he died, which in fact he did while still a young man.

The other brother, however, stayed where he was. By hard work and good deeds he did his best to win back the respect of the community. As the years passed people came to regard him as a man of integrity.

One day, many, many years after the branding, when he was old and important, a stranger to the town asked one of its younger inhabitants what the letters 'ST' on the forehead of the old gentleman who owned the town's biggest store meant.

'I can't remember the details,' answered the resident, 'but I think they are short for Saint.'

LOVE, COURTSHIP, WEDDING

330. The bashful boy got no nearer to his girl, made no attempt to hold her hand as the train in which they were

travelling plunged into a long, dark tunnel. Instead he said: 'This tunnel cost a hundred thousand pounds.'

Bored, fed-up and frustrated the girl retorted: 'And for all the good it's doing me it was a waste of money!'

331. 'Wen you're a married man, Samivel, you'll understand a good many things as you don't understand now; but vether it's worth while goin' through so much to learn so little, as the charity-boy said ven he got to the end of the alphabet, is a matter o' taste.' (Old Weller.) *(Pickwick Papers.) Charles Dickens.*

332. 'Allow me to congratulate you on today. I'm sure you'll look back on it as the happiest day of your life,' said a henpecked husband to his nephew one morning.

'But, uncle, I'm not getting married until tomorrow,' retorted the young man, thinking his uncle must have been out on the town the night before and had not yet got over it.

'I know that!' said his uncle bitterly.

333. Saw a wedding in the church ... and strange to see what delight we married people have to see these poor fools decoyed into our condition. *Samuel Pepys.*

334. A man was boasting to his friend about his tropical holiday.

'It had everything, Bill,' he said. 'Sleepy lagoons for me, sunny beaches for the wife – and sharks for her mother.'

335. Two men were talking about their wives.

'She's got a neck!' stormed Tom about his wife Joan. 'Fancy telling your Mary that she's made a man of me!'

His friend puffed up his chest and grinned condescendingly: 'You'd never hear my Mary doing that!'

'No,' Tom agreed solemnly. 'But I have heard her say she'd done her best.'

336. The sailor had taken the same girl out throughout his leave. The more he saw of her, the more he liked her. And the more difficult it was for him to control his passion. One evening after a long and tantalizing kiss he gasped: 'Mary, darling, let's get married or something.'

Mary pushed him away and regarded him quizzically:

'We'll get married,' she said, decisively.

337. A good wife should resemble three things. She should be like the town clock – keep time and regularity. She should not, however, like the town clock speak so loudly that all the town may hear. She should be like a snail – prudent and keep within her own house; she should not, however, be like a snail and carry all she has on her own back. She should be like an echo – speak when spoken to, but she should not be like an echo – determined always to have the last word.

338. 'Daddy, you'll simply love Harry,' enthused the girl who was home for Christmas from her work in a distant town. She paused a moment, the love light in her eyes, then went on: 'We might be getting engaged soon.'

'Has he got any money?' asked her father.

'Funny, Daddy!' She frowned, 'He asked just that about you.'

339. You think that you are Ann's suitor; that you are the pursuer and she the pursued; that it is your part to woo, to persuade, to prevail, to overcome. Fool: it is you who are the pursued, the marked-down quarry, the destined prey. *G. Bernard Shaw (Man & Superman.)*

340. 'Who introduced you to your wife?' asked a newly-married man at the golf club of another who looked henpecked.

The other shook his head: 'We just happened to meet. I don't blame anyone!!'

341. 'Paddy,' said his wife, 'our silver wedding is on Tuesday. Oughtn't we to kill the pig for it?'

Paddy shook his head and exclaimed in horror: 'By the Saints, why murder the poor innocent pig for something daft which happened twenty-five years ago?'

342. 'If I were your wife,' stormed the bachelor's sister-in-law, 'I'd poison you.'

'If you were my wife,' he retorted maliciously, 'it would be a pleasure to take it.'

343. Englishman: 'Ever been in love?'

Scot: 'Yes, often – I wish I had all the money.'

PADRE, PRIEST

344. A parson who was addicted to collecting stories and using them to illuminate his sermons was telling a colleague that his sister, who looked after him, was critically ill and he feared that there was little hope for her. 'Wonderful woman, you know,' he remarked, 'she's nearly a saint.'

Some months passed before they met again. When they did the sister had died. 'Great loss,' said her brother, reminds me of the story of a man who was persuaded to turn his dog into a greyhound. He was advised to give it two potatoes, the size of golf balls a day, together with an ounce of salt; and this was to be its only food. This was to continue for a fortnight, at the end of which period he was to reduce the diet to one potato and an ounce of salt a day. At the end of the second fortnight he was to reduce the diet still further – this time to half a potato a day and an ounce of salt. And by the end of this time it should start to look like a greyhound.

Six weeks later the man who owned the dog and the fellow who had given him advice met again. The man who had given the dietary advice at once asked about the dog, whether the diet had been tried.

'Yes,' nodded the dog owner. 'I did try it. And do you know it nearly worked. The dog was nearly a greyhound when it died.'

'And so,' went on the parson, 'with my sister, she was nearly a saint, but she died.'

345. Pat was dying and the priest was giving him the last rites. 'Say after me,' said the Priest, 'I renounce the devil and all his evil deeds.'

Pat said not a word, so the priest repeated what he had said.

Again Pat said nothing, and the priest tried again but with the same result.

Puzzled, the priest gave him a gentle shake. 'What's the matter?' he asked. 'Can't you hear me?'

'Sure I can hear you,' answered Pat. 'But don't you think this is the wrong time for me to antagonize anybody?'

346. A lawyer who was fond of the good things of life was put to sit next to a hot-gospelling, temperance minister at an official dinner.

When the meal was over the waiter came up to him to ask what he'd have to drink with his coffee.

'Oh, a brandy, please,' said the lawyer.

The waiter then turned to the bigoted minister: 'And would you like a brandy too, sir?'

'I'd rather commit adultery,' hissed the minister.

At once the lawyer retorted: 'Cancel my brandy, I didn't realize there was a choice.'

POLITICS

347. A heckler at a political meeting accused the speaker of being two-faced.

'Ladies and gentlemen,' said the speaker in hurt tones, 'I appeal to you. If I had two faces would I be wearing this one?'

348. A candidate for a seat on a Welsh County Council was asked at one of his political meetings whether he approved of the opening of public houses on Sunday or not. He realized at once that no matter which side he took he would lose votes on this highly controversial matter, and so for a moment or two was nonplussed. Then he smiled.

'Some of my friends,' he said, 'are all for Sunday opening. And some of my friends are against it. I want you to know, ladies and gentlemen, that I always stand with my friends!'

349. 'What's a political traitor, Daddy?' asked the small boy.

'A man who leaves our party,' answered the father, 'and goes over to another.'

'Then what's a man who leaves another party to come over to ours, Daddy?'

'A convert, my boy, a convert!'

PUBLIC SPEAKING, CHAIRMAN

350. A minister of religion was sad to see that only one man had turned up for his service, so instead of starting

forthwith he went up to the man and asked: 'As you're the only one here do you think I ought to go on with the service?'

The man answered: 'I don't know very much about such things but if I were a shepherd and one of my sheep wanted feeding, I'd feed him.'

The minister returned to the pulpit and went through the whole service, including a long sermon.

When it was over he returned to the man and asked him how he had done.

'Well,' said the man, 'I don't know very much about such things but if I had only one sheep in my whole flock I wouldn't throw him the whole load.'

351. Sir Winston Churchill rehearsed his speeches at every opportunity he had.

One morning while he was having his bath his valet heard his voice above the splashing and opened the door to ask 'Were you speaking to me, Sir.'

Sir Winston was obviously annoyed at the interruption so answered brusquely, 'No, I was addressing the House of Commons.'

352. In a speech, in London, Benjamin Disraeli described Gladstone, as 'A sophistical rhetorician, inebriated with the exuberance of his own verbosity.'

353. When a new Member of Parliament asked Mr Disraeli whether he should often take part in the debates the Prime Minister told him that he thought not, that it was much better for the House to wonder why he didn't speak than why he did.

354. The after-dinner speeches and the introductions had all been far too long. Everyone was bored including the last speaker whose turn it now was. He got up and yawned.

'Ladies and gentlemen,' he began, 'I have been asked to give you an address.' He looked around his tired audience most of whom looked fed up with it all, and smiled. 'Well,' he went on, 'the address is Richmond Hill and with your permission and indulgence that is where I am now going. Good night.'

355. An after-dinner speaker who was new to the art stood up and having suitably saluted his audience stopped dumbfounded. Presently, however, he composed himself sufficiently to say: 'A few hours ago only the Lord and I knew what I was going to say ... But now the Lord only knows!'

RESOURCEFUL

356. The door was opened for the insurance collector by a small boy. 'Is your mother in, Sonny?' he asked.

'No, she's out.'

'Your father, then?'

'No, he's out too.'

'Well, it's near dinner-time. I'll come in and wait by the fire.'

The boy shook his head: 'You can't, that's out too.

357. A man who had drunk well but not wisely hired a taxi to take him home. When he was approaching his destination he discovered that he had not got sufficient money to pay his fare. At that moment they were passing a coffee bar which was open. 'Stop!' he yelled to the driver, and got out. 'I won't be a moment,' he explained somewhat beerily to the driver, 'I've dropped a tenner somewhere in your taxi and can't find it in the dark. I'll get a box of matches here.'

As he entered the coffee bar he saw the taxi driver drive away.

358. When Christopher Columbus returned to Spain after having discovered America he was feted like a king. This made some courtiers jealous. One of them tried to embarrass Columbus at a banquet given in his honour. 'Are there no others who would have been capable of the enterprise if you had not discovered the Indies?' he asked.

Columbus did not answer directly. Instead he picked up an egg and invited those present to stand it on its end.

Of course, they all failed. 'Give it to me,' said Columbus. When they had done so, he struck its end on the table so that it broke, and stood the egg up.

'Now that I've shown you the way,' he remarked, 'any one of you can make an egg stand on its end. Similarly, now that I've shown you the way to the New World it is easy to follow.'

359. A woman went into a butcher's shop where six dressed chickens were exposed for sale. 'Pick the toughest three of these will you?' she asked the butcher. 'You see I keep lodgers.'

The butcher gladly did as she had asked him.

'Thank you,' she said, 'now I'll take the other three, if you please!'

SECRET

360. Two friends who had not seen one another for some time met in the street.

'You're looking very gloomy,' said one. 'Aren't you well?'

His friend shook his head. 'It's not that,' he answered. 'To tell you the truth I'm terribly worried these days.'

'What's the trouble?' asked his friend.

'Well, you remember my telling you I'd got a man to look up my family tree?'

'Yes.'

'He did so!' He sighed heavily: 'And now I'm having to pay him hush money.'

361. At the Youth Club the guest speaker, who was one of the town's wealthiest men, ended his address by saying, 'And now would you like to ask me a question?'

A tall young man named Andrew got up. 'Please, Sir,' he said, 'you said you've worked very hard all your life and we believe that. Then you said you've always been thrifty and always saved money. Surely, sir, you must sometimes have felt like having a spending spree, a blow-out, being extravagant.'

The businessman smiled, 'Of course, I have. But then I'd ask myself four questions. And they've saved me a lot of money. I still ask them.

First, before I buy I ask my self, 'Do you really want it?' I can usually say Yes to that one. Then I ask, 'But do you need it?' A lot fall down on that. My next question is, 'Can you afford it?' That one pulls me up sharply.

And finally I ask myself, 'But can you manage without it?' The few that survive that question are pretty essential.

SERVICES

362. Sylvia was talking to her R.A.F. brother after a party they had attended. 'I think Flying Officer Smith is wonderful,' she said. 'And all the things he's done – they're fab.'

'Really!' Her brother's voice was pained: 'You know Sylvia, the worst flyer and the best talker of all the birds is the parrot.'

SMOKING

363. A foreigner had gone back to his own country after extensive travel on British Rail. 'Trains in England are quite unlike those anywhere else' he told his listeners. 'Why, they have carriages for anything and everything. I have seen carriages not only labelled, Smoking, but Reading, Bath, Sandwich and many others.

364. Mrs. Smith had been carrying on to her husband for almost an hour on the deleterious effects to their health risked by people who smoked, and now was finally dwelling upon his unsuccessful attempts to stop.

'There's only one way to stop,' she concluded, 'Just stop, no ifs and no buts.' (Butts)

365. Mrs. Smith was enjoying her matutinal gossip with her next door neighbour and had, at last, got on to her favourite topic – finding fault with her son-in-law.

'Last night', she went on, 'he confessed he smokes forty cigarettes a day, and when I told him he must be mad, that even he must know that cigarettes are a health hazard – he must have seen that in the papers. D'you know, he turned on me and said 'I keep reading so much tripe about the bad effects which smoking is supposed to have on us that I've decided to give up – reading!'

SPORT

366. It was not the Caddie Master's best day. After an indifferent lunch he returned to the links to find a new caddie idling his time away.

'Jump to it,' he shouted. 'Don't stand about looking stupid and doing nothing as though you were a member of the club!'

TOASTS

367. The origin of clinking glasses before toasting friends is to be found when poisoning was all too common. To make sure that the drink you were given contained nothing harmful the custom grew of pouring a little into the glass of the person who handed it to you. As the glasses touched so they clinked. Today the people with whom we drink are much more trustworthy. Indeed most of them are a little shocked when they are told the origin of the clinking of glasses.

368. A Chinaman returning home from a holiday in England complained that we had peculiar customs. 'They,' he said to a friend, 'put a lump of sugar in a glass to make a drink sweet then add lemon to make it sour. They put in gin to warm themselves up and then ice to make themselves cool. Afterwards they say, "Here's to you," but drink it themselves.'

WOMEN, WIFE

369. God Made the World and rested;
         God made Man and rested;
      Then God made Woman,
         And ever since then
      Neither God not Man has rested!

370. Here's to God's first thought, Man!
      Here's to God's second thought, Woman!
      Second thoughts are always best,
      So here's to Woman!

INDEX TO EPIGRAMS, STORIES
AND ANECDOTES

In this list, the number given after each theme title refers to the number of the relevant epigram, story or anecdote – not the number of the page on which it may be found.